This book is dedicated to my wife, Colleen, my soul mate.

PHYSICIAN

Heal

THYSELF

Nearly Dead and the
Journey Back to Health

By Michael J. Hession, MD, FACC, FACP
Foreword by Nomi Levy-Carrick, MD
Afterword by Colleen A. Hession, RN

ISBN Paperback: # 979-8-9909866-0-2
ISBN Electronic: # 979-8-9909866-1-9
Library of Congress Control Number: # 2024914171

Author Headshot: Hayward Photography
Publishing Consultant: PRESStinley, PRESStinely.com

Printed in the United States of America.

Michael J. Hession
www.AcknowledgeAcceptAdapt.com

The names of the caregivers have been changed and are fictional. Use of names of family, friends, and physicians have been used with their permission.

The author's intent is only to offer information of a general nature to help you in your quest for emotional, physical, and spiritual well-being. In the event you use any of the information in this book for yourself, the author and the publisher assume no responsibility for your actions. This publication is not intended as a substitute for the advice of a healthcare professional.

Table of Contents

Prologue

Homebound, I was recovering from hip replacement surgery when the COVID-19 pandemic began to shake the world. Towards the end of 2019, reports from Wuhan, China, circulated, initially online then later in medical journals, of a new, potentially fatal viral infection. Pneumonia and a high mortality rate characterized this illness. Those who felt this was an issue solely for the Chinese were mistaken.

In 2002, the first severe acute respiratory syndrome (SARS) or SARS-CoV-1 was discovered in Asia. It peaked in 2003. Following the widespread adoption of masks, contact tracing and quarantines, by 2004, this outbreak had disappeared. Worldwide, there were 8,000 cases of SARS-CoV-1, approximately 800 deaths and, remarkably, only 29 confirmed cases in the U.S.A. The 2020 illness was found to be caused by a new strain of coronavirus known as SARS-CoV-2 or COVID-19. It was hoped that this version of the virus would be quickly defeated with similar measures as SARS-CoV-1. This time, hope was not a successful strategy.

By early 2020, the pandemic that scientists had hypothesized would happen surprised the globe. Worldwide public health measures quickly became overwhelmed. Hospitals were challenged to care for the volume of sick and dying from COVID-19. The virus spread exponentially as presciently described in the 2011 movie *Contagion* and left the world at its mercy. There was no mercy.

Unlike the 1918 influenza pandemic, which disproportionately killed the young (including my grandmother, then a 25-year-old Irish immigrant), COVID-19 first took the elderly, those with chronic illnesses, and the disadvantaged.

Cynics with little compassion referred to this as the natural culling of the herd.

A minority of countries, seeing that public health measures did little to abate the contagion, took the approach of letting the virus spread with the hope that natural selection would lead to "herd immunity." In theory, this would occur when approximately 70 percent or more of the population developed resistance to the virus from antibodies. This didn't prove true for COVID-19. It is common for viruses to mutate, and COVID-19 mutated rapidly. Like a deadly game of Whac-A-Mole, the virus spread to all fifty states and throughout the world, only to resurface in recurrent waves. Many, even the young, who survived the first and subsequent variations of the virus, succumbed to evolving strains. COVID-19 continues to circumnavigate the globe, exacting a staggering toll—even in countries which thought they had it defeated.

In the medical community, there was an uneasy feeling that this virus had the potential to be the dreaded worldwide catastrophe, similar to the 1918 flu pandemic, smallpox, and plagues that ravaged our planet centuries earlier. Unfortunately, too many pandemic false alarms had made world governments skeptical. SARS-CoV-1, MERS, and Ebola, though terrifying, never really spread across the globe. The 2009 H1N1 influenza died out. Hence, vaccine and treatment research faltered as the billion-dollar-plus price tag to treat something that would probably also extinguish itself naturally became too large a financial hurdle for Big Pharma and small biotech companies to overcome.

Complacency gradually replaced the spirit of preparedness that the World Health Organization (WHO) had built. Research on medications to fight viral illnesses and create vaccines were dialed back. This was a short-sighted decision. Although billions of dollars had been spent on finding an AIDS vaccine to no avail, effective antiviral therapies *had* been discovered, which transformed AIDS into a treatable, chronic disease.

Prologue

The news media provided around-the-clock coverage of hospitals, city morgues, and funeral homes overflowing their capacities. The dystopian horror of the ever-growing lines of refrigerated trucks acting as temporary morgues for victims of the pandemic gave a sense of the scale of death the world had not seen in over a century. Makeshift funeral pyres cremating the dead became so common in some areas of the world, a shortage of wood to fuel the flames became a concern.

I was left with a sense of hopelessness as I moved around with my walker, unable to help in this devastating crisis. It was after watching a nightly news report that I was struck by a particularly compelling story of a middle-aged man on life support, critically ill from COVID-19 and near death, when I realized that I did have something to offer: my own experience.

In 2014, I developed a viral infection that morphed into pneumonia, followed by the near-fatal complication of acute respiratory distress syndrome (ARDS), requiring mechanical life support. The story of what I went through, my unique perspective as both a patient and a physician, who not only survived but recovered, may be of help to those afflicted with this horrible illness as well as their families.

This is my first book, and it is the deeply personal account of my illness, survival, and recovery, along with the strategy I used to rebuild my life. In so doing, I became a better person and a better physician. My hope is that these words will help those whom I cannot directly care for.

Foreword

As medical interventions have become more effective at saving lives, we have had to turn attention to the long-term functional impacts of survivorship. What happens after a patient is discharged from the hospital? What does recovery from critical illness look like? Michael Hession sets out to describe his journey in a very personalized account that is part memoir, part how-to guide.

Dr. Hession's practice pre-illness was in some of the very care settings he later found himself as a patient. He provides a vivid account of how medical trauma can occur and manifest—and the importance of addressing the impacts both physically and mentally directly. This is integral to overall healing. Dr. Hession, through this harrowing account of critical illness, delirium, hospitalization, and survivorship, travels a winding road from profound debilitation to post-traumatic growth and re-engagement as a physician, as well as husband and father. One is struck by the ways in which faith, meaning, and purpose have figured into his recovery, and the ways this narrative provides both vehicle and reflection for each of these.

Dr. Hessions's account aligns with many experiences I have both observed and helped navigate as a clinician—both as a psychiatrist who was embedded in the medical ICU for over two years and as an outpatient clinician who ponders the neuropsychiatric dimensions of trauma-informed care across the health care system. By describing some of the strategies that have been effective in his recovery, Dr. Hession allows the reader an opportunity to learn a bit about the "what" of the approach and the "how" as it applies to his experience. In so doing, it may provide a hopeful roadmap for many of the millions who have survived critical illness.

Nomi C. Levy-Carrick, MD, MPhil
Assistant Professor of Psychiatry, Harvard Medical School

Chapter 1

The Light

*"Do not go gentle into that good night. Rage,
rage against the dying of the light."*
Dylan Thomas

Was I awake, or was I locked in a dream? My head felt foggy, or more precisely, the feeling was as though my brain was detached from the rest of my body. This made no sense. My next memory was of a shining, bright light. Not like when you wake from a nap to feel the warm summer sun on your face kind of light. This light had no warmth. Neither was it like cold winter sun on your face when you lay dazed in the snow after a fall when skiing. This light had a harsh bluish tinge, and it bore directly into me—deliberate and menacing. The light confused and unsettled me. Where was I?

There was no context. No memory of going anywhere to give me an idea of where I was or how I got here. The unsettled feeling gave way to panic. I couldn't speak. I couldn't move. Without my glasses, my vision was blurred. I couldn't see where I was. The possibility that this was just a bad dream that I would awaken from comforted me for an instant, but this was no dream. Disorientation washed over me. My heart was pounding, my mind raced, and my thoughts were jumbled. My mouth was dry, but I could taste the unmistakable sour taste of fear.

In rapid succession, panic gave way to terror—the wet yourself, soil yourself, elemental terror that I had never before experienced. All rational thought was lost as I began to ride a wave of recognition that I might be dead or dying. In this foggy haze, I remembered reading stories of people who had survived near death and recalled their descriptions of seeing a bright light. I struggled to understand what was happening. Deep down, I knew that death and near death are often unforeseen events that we have no agency or control over.

At the same time, belief and denial that this could be happening *to me* raged in my head. I could not think logically. My mind exploded. Like an unsynchronized cluster of fireworks, my thoughts randomly zoomed by, too rapidly to focus upon. But all were tinged with unmitigated horror. Emotions swept through me. I knew I was no longer in control of any part of my life. My brain screamed, "I am not ready to die," but no words came out. My life was slipping away no matter how hard I fought to stay alive.

Disembodied sounds were the next thing that I remember. Voices. But these voices seemed ephemeral. Was I losing my mind? Had I lost my mind? Or was I trapped in a nightmare I couldn't wake from? The voices weren't loud but were easily heard as if meant to be. They were unintelligible, neither anxious nor hushed. Rather, the voices were intense and sounded purposeful. They came rapidly from far away, then closer, louder; then they surrounded me. This was followed by the sensation of hands on my face. Oddly, the hands did not feel like skin. Nothing seemed real. Everything was happening too fast to understand or process.

I felt my body resist. My muscles became rigid, and I lost whatever semblance of control over my body I previously had. There was a sensation of something being placed inside my throat. I didn't know what was going on but was vaguely aware that whomever was doing this was skilled and fast. What happened next was my first haunting experience of many such events. The feeling was something one could never get used to or forget. I had never experienced torture, but this seemed as though it could be considered torture: the air was being sucked out from inside of me. What was left of my life force was being violently extracted, just as in the scene from the 2001 Brendan Fraser movie *The Mummy Returns,* when Imhotep inhales the life from the grave robbers, killing them. I felt my entire body go into spasm. Then things went black. Time stopped.

What had just happened was the first of many treatments called suctioning. In my terror, I was fighting or "bucking the ventilator." In proper medical terms, I experienced patient ventilator asynchrony. Pneumonia causes thick mucus secretions that clog the airways and prevent oxygen from efficiently getting into the bloodstream. If this problem isn't rapidly corrected with suctioning, vital organs would be deprived of that life-sustaining oxygen, and as the organs fail, death occurs. This was the most unpleasant treatment I had to endure, but enduring it was essential to survival. As a physician, I was always humbled by the suffering that people could withstand in order to survive, but everyone has their breaking point. Now it was my turn to find my limits of endurance. The treatments were random and unrelenting. Suctioning left me drenched in sweat and exhausted. If I was dead and in hell, then this was the beginning of an eternity of unimaginable torment.

When I awoke, I was still wet with perspiration and aware of heavily accented words spoken nearby. The words were hard to understand, but I had heard them before. Wait! What? In that instant I realized that a priest was reciting the Last Rights of the Roman Catholic Church, the final sacrament given to the dying. The inescapable conclusion was that these words were for *me.* It was me who was dying. None of this made sense. What had happened to me?

Next, I heard a different voice. The soft and familiar sound of my wife Colleen speaking into my left ear. I could feel the emotion in her voice, but her words were steady and clear. She

3

was holding back tears, knowing what I needed to hear without my even asking the questions. After 32 years of marriage, she could truly read my mind.

I was in the Medical Intensive Care Unit at Brigham and Woman's Hospital in Boston with serious pneumonia. It had started with a simple cough the week before Christmas, 2013. I had a common viral infection, but slowly, relentlessly, my condition deteriorated like a runaway freight train. The winter cough was followed by a fever, then shortness of breath, which deteriorated into pneumonia. The pneumonia was complicated by acute respiratory distress syndrome (ARDS). I was, in fact, actively dying and extremely close to death.

An ambulance had driven me from home to the Emergency Department of South Shore Hospital where I had worked for 29 years. Upon arrival, I was near death. The lung imaging and lab work confirmed the worst, that without heroic life support, I would not survive. After I arrived in the intensive care unit (ICU), I was rapidly placed on life support, as I could no longer adequately breathe on my own. This was the same ICU where I had cared for many patients; but for my own treatment, nothing was working. I was slipping away. Close to my head, the voices of two women in the background spoke of me in the past tense. This made no sense. I tried to say, "I am still here!" but no words came out. The critical care attending told my wife there was nothing further that could be done for me; I was dying. The critical care team recommended that I be transferred to a tertiary hospital where I could be considered for ECMO (extracorporeal membrane oxygenation), an artificial lung, reserved for patients who fail maximal life support on mechanical ventilation.

I was accepted as a patient in the Brigham ICU. Med Flight was activated. The window of opportunity to get me urgently required help narrowed as my health deteriorated. The situation was tense but about to become worse: the weather was changing, and a major winter blizzard was en

4

route to Boston. My survival depended on getting transferred ahead of the storm. Then, the crushing news came that the helicopter was grounded: the treacherous winter weather made it unsafe to fly. The Boston Med Flight Team decided to transport me via Advanced Life Support ground ambulance while the roads were still passible. Though risky, this transfer was felt to be my best chance. I was placed into a medically induced coma for the trip to BWH, where I arrived safely but nearer to death than life.

What happened next, I will never forget. After another suctioning treatment, things again went dark. This time, I don't recall waking the way I did after the prior treatments. Things were still black, but this time I became aware of crying in the distance. Where was the sound coming from? It became more intense and was nauseatingly familiar; the sound I remembered was "keening." This is an Irish word derived from the Gaelic "caoineady": the sound of intense, mournful wailing after the death of a loved one. The first and only time I heard this cry of desolation was at age 13, the night that my mother died. My father, brothers, sister, and even our dog made this anguished sound, which went on for hours, possibly days. Keening only meant one thing: death of a loved one. I could not understand why I was hearing this. The sound meant death; it meant I was dead!

My mind could not accept this. The crying unnerved me. I felt cold inside as warmth left my body but I did not shiver. The keening grew louder. I could not see who was making these sorrowful sounds or where they were coming from. Gradually, I felt myself floating into the darkness. I felt hands reaching out to grab me. There were many hands; some were very strong, but a more powerful force gently pulled me away. The keening quieted as the distance grew.

Somehow, I was able to glimpse the otherworldly, grief-contorted faces of my wife, sons, brothers, and sister. They were reaching out in desperation, trying to pull me back.

Their faces stained with tears and almost unrecognizable. It was then that I realized that the dolorous weeping was coming from my family, but that made no sense. They were trying to pull me back, but from where? My mind could not accept the possibility that I was dead.

I didn't feel dead, but what did I know about what death felt like? I tried to call to them but couldn't make any sound. Then, the faces and voices of my wife and family disappeared into nothingness. I tried desperately to hold on to the image of their faces. The inescapable reality was that I *must* be dead. Time and space were no longer dimensions. I was left floating, silently, in the black void. This sensation remained, as if I were being gently pulled in a direction that I couldn't see. It seemed to go on forever, but that was not possible. The sensation of floating was strangely peaceful and most surprisingly, I no longer felt afraid.

At some point, I became aware of a light. Not the harsh, blue-tinged hospital light that I first remembered. A light neither foreboding nor menacing. It was shimmering and drew me forward. The light filled me with the most peaceful feeling I had ever known. It was warm and calming. As I drew closer, the light took on the shape of a woman clothed in a luminous robe hovering above me. The sensation was rapturous and enveloped me.

Words that I will never forget came next: "Michael, it is not your time. You must go back. There is much to do." The image drifted away as I continued to float. She seemed familiar, but I don't know how this could be. A sense of inner peace permeated me. Even though I knew deep down that something bad had happened to bring me to experience near death, I was not dead. It was not my time to die. There is no way to quantify this period of time. It could have been seconds, hours, or even days. In the end, this thought was irrelevant as time stood still.

My floating reverie came to an end when I heard a soothing voice in my left ear, followed by the gentle touch of a hand on my face. Colleen. With certainty, at that moment, I understood this was not a dream, and I was definitely alive! She had great news. The critical care team at BWH had just told her that my blood oxygen levels were getting better, that my pneumonia was responding to treatment, with sustained, objective signs of improvement. The joy in the room was intoxicating. I would not need ECMO, and furthermore, they were dialing back the settings on the ventilator.

My own joy was enhanced by recognizing that the voice and image of the woman in the luminous robe…stayed with me.

What I was about to learn was just how hard it is to be a patient, to fight back from major illness and start over. I was trained to be a physician, not a patient. The fight would be arduous and take years. My struggle would launch me onto a roller coaster of emotions and a second near-death experience. At that moment, the shape my life would take was impossible to discern, but it was likely to be different than the one I knew. My future was uncertain. Strangely, from that point on, I did not fear death despite the horrors that awaited me.

Chapter 2

I Can Hear You

"The most important thing in communication is hearing what isn't said."
Peter Drucker

Fragments of memories came back as I recovered. I drifted in and out of consciousness over the eleven days that I was intubated in the BWH MICU. Each day, I heard different voices talking about me. The familiar voices of my wife; my sons, Michael and Patrick; along with those of my brothers, James and Paul; and my sister Maureen were clearly audible and comforting as they talked among themselves and to me. The medical team discussed my status at the foot of my bed near the doorway to the room. My wife answered the medical team's questions and later relayed the questions and answers to me.

There was a great deal of concern on the part of my physicians when delving into my travel history. My wife related a weeklong stay in Haiti in May of 2013, as part of a medical missionary trip to Saint Rock. Our conditions were primitive in Haiti when compared to America or Europe. However, they were luxurious beside those of the patients who traveled for hours in the dark of night, climbing down from remote mountain villages where they lived (without running water or sanitation), to be treated. We could hear their hushed voices talking as they began to arrive at dawn. We cared for hundreds of patients each day, many with untreated infections and myriad illnesses. The BWH infectious disease specialists were concerned that I might have contracted some rare illness. Tubes of blood were drawn for cultures that might reveal the organism attacking my lungs. A camera (bronchoscopy) was carefully and skillfully placed into my lungs to look for clues as well as to obtain cultures from inside my lungs' depths. Countless X-rays and CT scans were performed. Finally, it was determined that there was no infection from Haiti that had caused my condition. The cultures were negative. What brought me to near death was a common virus.

As I slowly improved, sedation and pain medication were cut back so that I would be able to better breathe on my own. Sedatives and opioids depress normal breathing, and overdoses of these medications lead to cessation of breathing—death. Weaning me off the ventilator and life support would be a painstakingly slow process with many difficult days ahead. With less sedation and pain medication, my brain was able to comprehend more of what was happening, though my eyes remained closed.

For example, in order to prevent skin breakdown, my position had to be changed several times a day. This was no easy task and required several people to accomplish: I was dead weight, hooked up to my life support machines and IVs, with tubes and wires going everywhere. One day, after the staff changed my position from my back to lying on my left side, the pain in my left hip was excruciating, but I could not speak to tell them or move on my own. I was supposed to have had elective surgery to replace my worn-out left hip the first week of January 2014. However, my life took an unexpected turn. The pain was hard to bear. At some point, my wife came into the room, instantly saw the agony on my face, realized that I was lying on my left hip, and knew what had to be done. Shortly thereafter, the staff changed my position, and the pain resolved. This was a teaching moment for everyone.

At the time of this health crisis, my wife and I had been married for 32 years. We could read one another's faces and knew what we were feeling. I could never hide anything; my face was an open book to her. She was very observant by nature, and reading body language was a skill she honed as a certified critical care medical ICU nurse (CCRN).

My family stayed with me 24 hours a day, taking shifts, and that was a good thing. My wife and family members took turns talking with me daily. They told me stories and what was going on in the world in the hope that I could hear them. I could hear but I could not communicate or move. I heard them speaking to the staff and each other. This was more than reassuring; it was my link to reality. My son Michael was in medical school and had come home from New York City when he heard I was near death. I recall hearing him tell his mother of his perilous trek through the raging blizzard to get to my ICU bed. Another winter tale I overheard was from my other son. Earlier in the year I had bought tickets to the "Frozen Fenway" hockey game between Boston College and Notre Dame. Patrick, who hates the cold, went with friends since I was otherwise occupied. After the game, I heard him say that "Frozen Fenway" was an apt description of the hockey game, as he nearly froze in the stands with the game-time temperature in the single digits without the wind chill.

Emotionally and psychologically, their presence and voices gave me strength. I now find it hard to understand why for so many years, family members were discouraged from staying with their loved ones in hospital ICUs. Fortunately, with the advent of patient-centered medical care and shared decision making, this is no longer the situation. Having someone you know and love speak to you or read to you when you are intubated is immeasurably calming and therapeutic. It also improves patient safety to a much larger extent than I ever could have imagined but was soon to find out. (Unfortunately, the COVID-19 pandemic abruptly changed this advance in patient well-being. Patient isolation was instituted in an attempt to prevent the spread of the virus and serve the greater good.)

One day, a form of brain wave testing, a bispectral index (BIS), was performed. The concept of "awareness while under anesthesia" was a known cause of PTSD in patients undergoing surgery. This technology provides an objective measure of the level of sedation under anesthesia and became widely used in operating rooms and ICUs. Brain monitoring systems provide clinicians critical information to determine the precise amount of medication warranted, to avoid over or under sedation. Following my test, the technician proclaimed, "He is still in there."

I frantically tried to scream, "I can hear you!" but to no avail.

This inability to be interactive in the normal human way gave staff and people in my room a misguided sense of confidentiality. It was strange how much private and highly personal information people spoke about because I was intubated and comatose. It's as though because you are inanimate, you're like a piece of furniture. From talking with others who have been in the same condition as I, my experience was not unique.

When it was quiet, I could have been floating in space or trapped in a cave. Keeping sane through this became a major concern alongside my constant worry about what was going on with me medically. For the first time, as a physician, I had a deep understanding of how patients could develop ICU psychosis, an acute delirium that is very stressful for the patient to experience and difficult for family members to witness. Fortunately, most patients have little to no memory of this, and unlike PTSD, it has a much shorter duration.

As the dosages of medication used to sedate me continued to be decreased (to wean me off the ventilator), I began to detect the rhythms of the day. Very early in the morning the phlebotomists came by to draw blood. This was done first thing so the results would be available to the ICU team when they rounded several hours later. The phlebotomists were quiet, as they performed their tasks when patients were usually asleep. Like ninjas, they silently entered the room. You'd know they were present when you felt the pressure of the tourniquet around your upper arm, followed by the sensation of the cold antiseptic cleansing the inside portion of your elbow. The only words spoken were, "You're going to feel a little pinch," as the blood was removed from the vein. Then a bandage was placed on the area. The entire episode took only a few minutes. They left as silently as they came.

Other times during the process of weaning off the ventilator, respiratory therapy technicians drew a specialized test called an arterial blood gas (ABG). This procedure was significantly more uncomfortable but gave a precise reading of the oxygen and carbon dioxide levels of my blood, as well as the acid balance (pH). This information helped guide my ventilator settings. The respiratory therapists always introduced themselves even though I was intubated and could not respond. They explained what they were going to do and stated, "This will hurt." The skin on my lower arm at the wrist was cleansed with an antiseptic, followed by a second warning of, "This will hurt." After the ABG was drawn from my radial artery, pressure was placed to prevent any oozing, then a bandage was put on.

Even these brief one-way verbal exchanges soothed me when I was intubated. The sound of their voices, their compassion and professionalism, were comforting, but most important and immensely reassuring was their recognition of me as a sentient human being. Even though I was unresponsive and they had no way of knowing that I could hear them, they took the time to show me the same respect as for any other person whom they were caring for.

Although this may sound odd, I didn't mind these procedures, which would surprise anyone who knew me. It was no secret how much I hated to have my blood drawn. I used to be teased that, "I could dish it out, but I couldn't take it."

Most of what I remember is unpleasant, but there were some funny moments. Molly was one of my nurses. She was very methodical, and at the beginning of each shift she would stand inches from my face and speak in a firm, slow voice, syllable by syllable into my right ear. "This is Molly. I am your nurse." She would tell me the time, the day, and what she was going to do to me. She wore glasses with thick lenses that magnified her eyes. My vision was blurry without my glasses, giving Molly a distorted image and the appearance of a "bug-eyed" Mrs. Magoo. This image coupled with the slow cadence of her voice reminded me of a scene from *Alice in Wonderland*.

As is typical, I became constipated from the opioids and went on to develop abdominal pain. The physicians became alarmed at my tender abdomen and ordered a CT scan. In retrospect, this was my first episode of diverticulitis. Molly insisted to the medical team that I just needed to "poop." However, the team wanted tests. The CT scan results confirmed her observation. The medical team ordered laxatives and for the next few days, with her "bug eyes" nearly touching my face and her booming voice in my right ear, she'd say, "I told them you needed to poop."

In my mind, I responded to her. "I'm not even in control of my breathing let alone any other bodily function." It was so comical that for the first time I found something to laugh about even if I laughed inside. There were to be far too few days with laughter for a very long time.

Chapter 3

Staying Sane

"We are not here to curse the darkness, but to light the candle that can guide us to a safe and sane future."
John Fitzgerald Kennedy

Rachel Carson wrote, "There is something infinitely healing in these repeated refrains of nature, the assurance that after night, dawn comes." Unfortunately, the normal diurnal cues of day and night were no longer a part of my life. There was no comfort from waking up to the sun. The time that I spent sleeping and waking were fragmented, random periods that I had no ability to identify or quantify. Time no longer existed as a dimension. I had never experienced solitary confinement, but I had read Admiral Stockdale's description: it was the worst punishment that could be inflicted on a prisoner; it broke their sanity. Nothing in my life had prepared me for the mental and emotional stress of being intubated, sedated, and paralyzed. The indescribable feeling of inner peace that I had experienced earlier, of knowing that I was not going to die, was slowly replaced by the embryonic fear that something worse than death awaited me.

In high school, one of my favorite classes was literature. We studied Edgar Allen Poe, the well-known master of short-story horror. I remember being completely creeped out after reading two of his most famous tales: the "Cask of Amontillado" and "The Fall of the House of Usher." The theme he focused on in both was that of being entombed alive. He told the stories with such masterful skill that I doubt anyone who has ever read these tales did not experience the mental and visceral horror that they were meant to evoke. Being buried alive seemed to be one of the cruelest deaths imaginable. Never did it occur to me that I would experience this feeling, but I was actually living what he described. My death felt close, and I recall how the main character's enemy Fortunato in the "Cask of Amontillado" and the sister in "The Fall of The House of Usher" described their last moments. I was beyond terrified by what the future might hold.

During medical school training, I had cared for a stroke victim with "locked-in syndrome." The textbook description by Drs. Plum and Posner, however clinical, is accurate. In literature, Alexandre Dumas in *The Count of Monte Cristo* gives a romanticized depiction of this particular stroke syndrome in the character of Monsieur Noirtier de Villefort: "The mind alone is still active in this human machine." This type of stroke leaves you with an intact mind but near-complete paralysis of all muscles except those that control your ability to move your eyes. You can hear, think, feel, breathe, and experience emotion as well as pain, but you are unable to speak. Dumas went on to describe how Monsieur Noirtier de Villefort's grand-daughter, Valentine de Villefort, "…had resolved this strange problem, and was able to easily understand his thoughts and to convey her own in return." Love and devotion to her grandfather inspired her to learn to communicate with him. She learned to read the emotions he wished to convey by studying his face and communicated with him through his eye movements. I was exceptionally fortunate to have my wife Colleen as my Valentine.

Yet for hours, I was locked within my own world. When I was awake, I sang every verse of every song I could remember, mostly from the 1970s and 1980s, over and over in my head. I recited every poem I could recall. My favorite poem since childhood still remains Robert Frost's "Stopping by the Wood on a Snowy Evening."

Whose woods are these I think I know
His house is in the village, though;
He will not see me stopping here
To watch his woods fill up with snow.
My little horse must think it queer
To stop without a farmhouse near
Between the woods and frozen lake
The darkest evening of the year.

He gives his harness bells a shake
To ask if there is some mistake.
The only other sound's the sweep
Of easy wind and downy flake.

The woods are lovely, dark and deep,
But I have promises to keep,
And miles to go before I sleep,
And miles to go before I sleep

Even though I am a physician, a scientist, I have a deep faith. I said every prayer I could remember, especially to Saint Jude, the Patron Saint of hopeless causes, whom I was taught about as a child. I recited the Rosary over and over. The saying, "There are no atheists in foxholes," is attributed to the U.S. military chaplain, William Thomas Cummings, during a field sermon at the Battle of Bataan in 1942. From personal experience as a patient and as a physician, I would add that there are no atheists in ICUs. The need to pray was primal, and I did so every waking moment. Later, I learned that my family, my friends, as well as countless others remembered me in their quiet moments or during liturgical services. My wife had asked our church pastor to have the entire congregation pray for my recovery as I had done for others who were seriously ill. It had never occurred to me that someday my congregation would be asked to do the same for me. I had learned as a child that not all prayers are answered. Seeking God's healing power had failed to lead to my mother's recovery. This did not deter me, and the recitation of the words provided inexplicable comfort.

Despite this forced mental engagement, I felt at times as though I was losing my grip on reality. I had cared for patients who developed ICU psychosis and was afraid that I would succumb to this terrifying complication, horrific for family members, as well. It can take days to months for a patient to return to their baseline mental and emotional status. When I forgot a verse to a poem or song, I became agitated and fearful. I realized that I needed something more detailed to focus on that actively stimulated my thinking, rather than using rote memory to keep me sane.

One night, my brother Jim stayed with me and talked of the dream home he was building. That's what I decided to do: I would design my own dream home inside my head. This required exceptional active thinking that challenged me in a positive way. I no longer tried to remember the past but rather, I visualized my life in the future. Viktor Frankl wrote in his book, *Man's Search for Meaning*, "It is a peculiarity of man that he can only live by looking to the future." I agree.

My brother and I are very much alike. Born a little more than one year apart, we were similarly brought up and educated. We shared numerous life experiences; now I mirrored his activity of creating the ultimate place to live. In my mind, I chose the location: Cape Cod at the mouth of the Bass River. My home was constructed so that every room had a view of either the sun rising in the east or setting in the west. The afternoon south-westerly breeze would cool the house. I pictured a dock off the back with a sailboat, a Catboat, to cruise the waters off Cape Cod. The only problem was that I did not know how to sail. I supposed that, initially, my sons could take my wife and me aboard. Sailing lessons were added to the growing wish list of things that I had to make time "to do."

My wife loves to cook, so I fashioned a gourmet kitchen that looked out over the river into Nantucket Sound. I also built an outdoor cooking area, as Colleen enjoyed it when I was able to grill. These mental exercises consumed my waking time. The joyful, albeit demanding, all-consuming mental activity of designing this home, furnishing it room by room, imagining the landscape and the hardscape became my main mental occupation. The details of the three-dimensional process excited me and immersed my mind as deeply as a one-thousand-piece puzzle. It took me away from my painful reality. My training as a physician told me that if I spent too much time worrying about what could not be changed regarding my physical condition, I would be led down the "rabbit hole" of insanity.

When I wasn't involved inside my head with construction, I planned vacations that Colleen and I would take. We had scheduled a trip to spend April of 2014 in Paris to visit our son, Patrick, who was teaching in the South of France. This would not happen, but I promised myself to put it on my mental calendar for another time. Creating a waterfront homestead and imagining exotic trips made me feel happy and filled the hours. I could not change the past, was powerless over the present, so I focused on the future with gusto. The more daring, the better.

I recalled lessons learned at Boston College from the Greek Stoic philosopher, Epictetus, who survived slavery; from Viktor Frankl who survived Auschwitz; and Admiral Stockdale who survived eight years of torture interspersed with solitary confinement as a POW in North Vietnam. In varying traumatic life experiences, they all affirmed: How you respond to external forces that are not in your control is up to you—and is how you survive the unimaginable. How I reacted to the daily ebb and flow of medical updates was my choice, my decision.

Colleen quickly observed that I was more alert and started to help me communicate using a letter board. She placed my glasses on my face and would point to a letter. If it was part of the word that I wanted to say, I would blink my eyes (as did M. Noirtier de Villefort in the Count of Monte Cristo). Knowing that I could communicate was like being freed from prison. Tediously, but joyfully, we communicated in this way.

Without sedatives and opioids, the pain caused by the tube down my throat felt like razor blades deep inside of me. The possible need for a tracheostomy was discussed. Although I feared this procedure, the promise of relief from this unrelenting discomfort was enticing.

The ICU team was encouraged by the fact that I was improving daily even if by very small increments. They exhorted me to fight through the pain. The decision was made to hold off on having a tracheostomy and to continue with the process to get me off the respirator, however long it would take. To insure a successful wean, there would be minimal to no sedation or opioids that could suppress my breathing. The burning torment in my throat was constant and stretched my limits of endurance. This agony was unlike the random, episodic horror I had experienced with suctioning. It was unrelenting and felt like a garden hose covered in barbed wire had been placed down my throat into my windpipe. Days passed, and the tube eroded the back of my throat; the slightest movement resulted in spasms of pain.

Concentrating on anything became impossible as the constant torment overtook the coping mechanisms I had built. No longer was I able to focus on the details of building my dream home; physical misery overwhelmed my mind. It brought me to the brink of insanity, drowning out any other thoughts. My ICU team explained that if I was to breathe on my own, off the ventilator, I had to bear the pain. There was no other choice but to focus on the goal of getting off of life support.

Finally, the breathing tube was removed. I was able to hold my own with the help of non-invasive ventilation (BiPap). With this device, oxygen was forced into my lungs under pressure via a tightfitting mask that covered my face from the hairline of my forehead to under my chin. It was held in place by sturdy straps. The tube running from my mouth into my lungs was gone as was the pain. One by one, tubes were removed. Later, I learned that I had endured 11 days on life support in the BWH ICU, not counting the days at South Shore Hospital.

Once I proved that I could remain safely off the ventilator for over 24 hours, I was moved from the ICU to the step-down floor. Transferring to this "recovery" room was tangible proof that I was getting better. I was still unable to move any part of my body, but that wasn't my chief concern: my mind was totally focused on breathing. It was hard to believe that I needed to spend so much emotional and physical energy on the simple act of inhaling and exhaling, an automatic bodily function that for my entire life I had taken for granted.

Although elated to be out of the ICU, my first night was more eventful than I imagined it would be. Sometime during the night, I began to have serious trouble breathing. Still paralyzed, I did not have the use of my hands to activate the "Call Button," and my voice was barely audible from inside the face mask. I was helpless and felt as if I was being suffocated from drowning.

Fortunately, I was never alone—my wife, sons, or siblings still staying with me day and night. That evening, it was my son Patrick's turn. He quickly saw that I was in distress and went to notify the nursing staff and physicians. The fear of being intubated again, of being placed back on life support, was almost too much to comprehend, but I couldn't breathe, so it was a terrifying possibility. The memory of intubation was still raw.

After the physical examination, chest X-ray, and blood gases were finished, I was given IV medications. My oxygen and pressures were adjusted. Thankfully, within a short period of time, my breathing improved. The imminent danger passed, but the terror of this close call unnerved me and was slow to dissipate. From then on, a full night's sleep was a thing of the past. I gained first-hand insight into why so many patients over the years complained of trouble sleeping through the night after surviving major illness.

My wife had already saved my life; now my son had as well. My family saved me physically and emotionally. What a supreme blessing that they never left my side throughout my stay at Brigham and Women's Hospital. (Regretfully, the COVID-19-induced isolation has added emotional trauma to the physical pain that patients, families, nurses, therapists, and physicians have experienced and will take a long time to recover from.)

After several days of stability, my wife and I were informed that the case manager had decided that I was to go to a chronic care facility. She felt that I needed long-term care, as my return to independent living was unlikely to happen in the next month or possibly ever. My wife and I discussed this, and we refused. We were medical professionals and knew that my best chance for recovery was at an acute rehabilitation hospital, specifically Spaulding Hospital, one of the best in the country and a few miles from BWH.

It is important to understand that *surviving* ARDS was only the first step of my healing journey. Being cared for in a major academic medical center with an "A Team" of physicians, nurses, and therapists 24/7 vastly improved the odds of survival. However, without intense physical therapy at a facility with expertise in rehabilitation of patients recovering from critical illness, my chances of returning to an independent life were slim and close to zero. My physical therapist Nadine worked tirelessly to push for this, as did my nurses and physicians. Colleen channeled her strength into me unceasingly. I had to prove that I was strong enough to complete a minimum of three hours of demanding physical therapy, daily. I dug down deep to find a way to meet this daunting challenge. Without my wife, family, friends, colleagues, and the team of caregivers at BWH, this next chapter of my life would never have been written. Colleen and my Chief, Peter Grape, MD, unwaveringly advocated for me. Finally, word came that I was accepted at Spaulding Hospital!

Chapter 4

Paralyzed

"Find Your Strength."
Spaulding Hospital

When first admitted, I had been placed in a hospital gown and my clothes taken home by my wife. This is all I had worn throughout my stay. On the day of transfer to Spaulding Hospital, I was given the set of generic grey sweatpants and sweatshirt that the homeless receive at discharge. I was beyond grateful. Ambulance staff moved me from my bed to the stretcher for the beginning of what was to be a much longer and frightening chapter of my life. Although alive, and happy to be alive, my future was uncertain.

As it was the end of January, I felt extremely cold despite being bundled for the ride. The frigid air jolted me as I entered a new world I had never dreamed of. The ambulance drivers transported me to the sixth floor. I read the sign in disbelief: Spinal Cord Injury Unit. My total focus at BWH had been on my breathing. The reality that I had no movement from the neck down had not registered until that moment. My wife held onto my hand and talked me through the abject fear she knew was raging inside of me. This was my new reality. Overwhelmed, my mind again exploded into a kaleidoscope of terrifying thoughts. There was no understanding the ordeal that I had just survived. I simply could not wrap my head around it nor could I fully grasp what was now occurring This was a different type of terror from what I had recently experienced.

I lay motionless in my Spaulding Hospital bed, grappling with the awareness that I was going to learn what it was like to be a patient attempting to recover from paralysis and a critical illness. I realized that I had never, longitudinally, taken care of a patient in a similar condition. This put me on a par with non-medical patients, as I had no first-hand experience of what lay ahead, no reference point to guide me. My professional focus had been to care for acutely ill patients suffering from heart attacks, arrhythmia, and congestive heart failure. Rehabilitation medicine was neither a significant part of my training nor life experience.

With the benefit of glasses, my eyes surveyed the room and recognized that Spaulding Hospital was a new, state-of-the-art building. In large letters on the wall was a sign proclaiming its motto, "FIND YOUR STRENGTH." It was impossible not to notice; all their literature started with the same encouraging advice. Colleen remained, and staff arrived shortly to greet me. We were overwhelmed with the infectiously positive "you can do this" attitude that every member of the team exuded. Working for many decades in hospital settings from oncology to ICUs, we were impressed. It was obvious that the philosophy for staff was: If troubled with a personal issue, check your baggage at the door. I know this could not have come easily, but their mission was clear, and their focus on their patients was laser sharp.

When everyone had left, my wife looked out the window and noticed that in a vacant field directly across from my room, someone had written in the snow, "I love you," encircled with a giant heart. It was February and so cold, and the message stayed for weeks. When I was strong enough to stand by the window, I saw it. Someone really cared for a loved one, but everyone who saw this message must have felt the love as I surely did. Random acts of kindness are powerful.

Once the formalities of arriving at a new hospital were concluded, the teams came in—physical therapy, occupational therapy, and speech therapy—to assess my physical function and needs (which were many). Goals of care were established. Tests would be necessary to determine why I was paralyzed. Three possibilities raised were: critical care myopathy, an adverse reaction to prolonged chemical paralysis (with Norcurium), or Guillain–Barré syndrome. Recovery from each was about the same, six to twelve months. Given the similar prognosis and timeframe for recovery, the answer to what was going on was somewhat meaningless. Yet after a multitude of tests and evaluations, it was determined that I had a form of Guillain-Barré syndrome. Although uncommon, even rare, it is often preceded by a viral respiratory infection, such as I was recovering from, or a gastrointestinal illness. Symptoms of Guillain-Barré plateau after four weeks, but recovery can take months (or years). Some 80 percent of patients with this illness usually begin to walk independently six months after diagnosis. At least I now had a time frame to use as a metric for my recovery.

The next day, sequentially, physical therapy (PT), occupational therapy (OT), and speech therapy started in earnest. This is why you had to be able to devote a minimum of three hours of work to qualify for in-patient hospital rehabilitation. Each team had me for an hour a day with rest periods in between. Furtively, my eyes kept looking at the "Find Your Strength" sign. The reality was that I had no physical strength. I struggled with how I could find that which felt totally lost. The sign challenged every patient admitted to Spaulding Hospital.

PT stretched my tendons and ligaments, which, as a consequence of prolonged immobility (from my pneumonia and ARDS), had become contracted or shrunken. My muscles had atrophied. Stretching was much more painful than I could ever have imagined. I had seen highly trained football players being stretched out on the sidelines by professional trainers during games. What was happening to me was very different. My tendons and ligaments were not supple like those of an elite athlete. The large muscles of my back and thigh were in a constant state of painful spasm. The procedures to relieve the spasms were even more excruciating than the spasms themselves. Deep tissue massage and mechanical massage with specially designed, gleaming stainless-steel tools brought tears to my eyes but worked amazingly well. My therapists were extraordinarily skilled and expert at determining the amount of pain that I could withstand during these procedures.

During medical school anatomy class, I had learned that the human body has 640 muscles. The shocking reality was that all 640 muscles of my body had atrophied, and the tendons attached to them had contracted like old rubber bands. I had no idea how long it would take to regain strength in these muscles and return flexibility to my tendons. When I looked closely at my hand, it appeared skeletal, as if each small muscle had shriveled up. My fingers no longer moved no matter how hard I willed them to. My first night at Spaulding, I had to ask someone to scratch my nose, as this simple act was impossible.

Although I was hungry and malnourished, I could not be fed. Staff had quickly assessed that I could not safely swallow. It had only been a few days since I had re-learned how to breathe. I would also need to be taught how to eat again. Speech therapy was employed to retrain those muscles needed to swallow and to restore the coordination involved with the heretofore subconscious task. Relearning this turned out to be exceedingly more difficult than I expected.

The first foods allowed were nectar-thickened liquids which had the taste and consistency of old-fashioned wallpaper paste. This was slowly and painstakingly placed in my mouth. My tongue had to be retaught its role in swallowing. Food has to pass from the mouth (or pharynx) into the esophagus (food pipe), then into the stomach. The esophagus sits perilously close to the trachea, which leads to the lungs. Aspiration, or swallowing food down the wrong "pipe," is a common problem after prolonged intubation and critical illness. When this dreaded complication happens, it results in serious pneumonia, which could lead to repeat intubation and going back on the ventilator. This could also, potentially, be a fatal event.

I had to learn to eat and drink using the "chin tuck" position, which required me to place my chin on my chest before swallowing, to facilitate food sliding into my stomach and not my lungs. The paste was tediously spoon-fed into me until the speech therapists deemed that the muscle strength and coordination were adequate and I could be given soft solids. Eating solid food was my first victory at Spaulding Rehabilitation Hospital.

The task of rebuilding myself was Herculean. Each team was assigned an hour and they divided me up by muscle groups, each with a specific plan of rehabilitation and a timetable. Weekly goals to achieve were defined. I was given a book to document my progress and for my notes. It sat blank, as I could not use my hands to write. Formal therapy was for three hours a day, six days a week with Sundays off. I was expected to perform "homework" exercises in my free time. The schedule was exhausting, and I frequently needed to nap (several times a day), something I hadn't done since I was a small child.

After some time passed, I realized that what I did have was inner strength, a powerful desire to live, and an unlimited capacity for hard work. I adapted the hospital's motto to: "Find Your Inner Strength."

When I was strong enough, I was assigned increasingly difficult physical and occupational therapy exercises. After a few days of improvement, I worked up the courage to ask how long my rehabilitation would take. The response was that for every day in the hospital most people require at least one week of rehabilitation. I had spent over 14 days in the ICU and four more in the step-down unit. By that metric, a minimum of eighteen weeks of rehabilitation lay ahead. Later, however, I was told that recovery from ARDS and the complication of Guillain-Barré syndrome was expected to take up to a year or longer, and that it was as yet unknown what the extent of my own recovery would be. Except for testing, I had not been out of my hospital room at Spaulding. A daunting road lay ahead.

When I was not exercising, I was reading. I knew that I had to work on maintaining cognitive function. This was on me. My family and friends brought in motivational books and my medical journals, which I read voraciously. This supportive group ceaselessly worked to keep my emotional health in good shape, and of particular help was something unexpected.

After my first few days in Spaulding Hospital, Colleen started bringing in bags and bags of "Get Well" cards and letters from friends, family, and many of my patients. There were hundreds. I must admit, before this illness, I was never a person who sent out cards. If I wanted to say something, I would call or visit the person. This illness taught me many valuable lessons, and what these "Get Well" cards can mean for patients was one of the most surprising. When you are very sick and in the hospital for weeks, or in my case months, your world becomes compressed. The walls close in; the room gets smaller and smaller. "Get Well" cards, letters, and visits were uplifting. They reminded me that others really did care for me, that I was not forgotten, and most of all, that my life was meaningful to others and ultimately to myself. This connection inspired me to recover as much of my life as humanly possible, to go on when going on seemed too daunting.

I reread the cards countless times. Some were brief notes of encouragement while others were long, heartfelt stories thanking me for saving their lives. Others were from grateful family members of those whose lives I couldn't save but I'd helped ease the suffering of their loved ones, allowing death with dignity. There were so many deeply moving letters. They told me of how I had made a difference and touched me in a way I never dreamed of. They were a testament to the meaning of my life, how as a doctor I had helped others. They crystallized that being a physician was my life's purpose and that I had been given a second chance in life to continue to make a difference. I promised myself that I would find a way, in some capacity, to resume my practice. It always was, and remains, an honor and privilege to care for another human being.

It was humbling to be a patient and worrisome to imagine not doing what for decades had been my life. No one expected me to return to the practice of medicine. Several cards seemed like eulogies with patients explaining why they were choosing new physicians to care for them. It is much harder to be a patient than a physician. The odyssey of my illness and agonizing recovery provided me a very nuanced insight into the difference in the meanings of sympathy and empathy. The Webster dictionary describes sympathy as feelings of pity and sorrow for someone else's misfortune, and empathy as the ability to understand and share the feelings of others. I began to feel the difference in cards that expressed sympathy versus empathy. The empathetic notes resonated with knowing and hope. The sympathetic notes made me feel hopeless as though a chapter of my life was over.

When the day came that I was strong enough to sit in a wheelchair, I was taken to the gym. This was the small gym on the spinal cord floor that was a prelude to future grueling workouts. The simplest exercise took all the mental determination I could summon as well as all the physical strength I had. A few minutes of movement left me drenched with sweat and exhausted. Full recovery and independence seemed beyond comprehension. The staff were well aware that this was how patients felt at the beginning and knew exactly which motivating words to use. "If you work hard and don't quit, you will improve," inspired confidence and hope. Expectations they set were realistic but designed to challenge me to my utmost. There was no false hope and no sugarcoating anything.

My PT, OT, and speech therapists were relentless but in a positive and focused way. They pushed me to my capacity, much harder than I would have pushed myself, but never beyond what was safe and possible. These staff members acted like drill sergeants pushing raw recruits past what they thought were their limits to what they were capable of becoming. I remain forever grateful to these expertly skilled observers and trainers in the art and science of rehabilitative medicine who bring broken humans back to their best physical shape possible. Each day they helped me find inner strength to push forward.

My situation was hard to comprehend. I had not yet fully recovered from near death due to pneumonia. Almost every night I set off alarms when my oxygen level dropped. Sleeping on my back impeded my damaged lungs from fully inflating. Other positions were unsafe due to my paralysis. The nursing and respiratory staff would charge in, turning on the bright lights to be certain that I was okay. I was placed on continuous oxygen, which was extremely drying and repeatedly gave me a bloody nose. Even when my oxygen level was stable, I often woke with a night terror that I had stopped breathing. The staff would rush in to see what I was screaming about. One nightmare was so bad, the staff wanted to call my wife and ask her to come in to reassure me that I was still breathing adequately.

Therapies were taxing, but fragmented sleep made the exercises truly exhausting. With each experience, I more deeply understood the mental and physical challenges so many of my patients had faced when recovering from serious illnesses and why some never made it home from the chronic care facilities. I realized that if I wanted to rebuild my life, I had to avoid the trap of mourning the past or I wouldn't have access to enough of myself in the present. I'd wind up forfeiting the future. I had no idea what my new normal would be, but I knew that if I compared my life as it was now to what it was before ARDS, I would never reach my full potential.

After several weeks, I made incremental but measurable progress. I could swallow and was nutritionally improving. I was strong enough to sit up and had limited use of my hands.

One of my exercises was with elastic bands on my fingers that I had to move inward and outward to strengthen the atrophied muscles of my hands. Ironic, that in the past, I used to do that mindlessly, but no longer.

I was also trained on how to use an electric wheelchair. Actually, this was much harder for me than I expected. The controller was on the left, and I was right-handed. Intended as an exercise to improve the coordination of my non-dominant hand, there were two speeds: turtle and rabbit. My coordination was lacking, and after a few crashes, I was told not to use rabbit speed. My newfound mobility was intoxicating after being flat on my back for over a month. Another awareness: how liberating an electric wheelchair is if you are paralyzed.

One sunny winter day, my wife took me on a tour of the spinal cord floor. Up until that point I had not spent much time outside my hospital room. She pushed me down the long hallway, past the small gym and into the common family room which provided a beautiful vista of Boston Harbor and Charlestown from two sides. I found the view of the water peaceful. It reminded me of my happy place on Cape Cod. Though other patients were present with their families, the room was quiet, almost somber, with little interaction. Emotions were easy to read on the faces of those around me. They revealed shock and confusion from the effort of trying to understand the new reality of their lives and those of their loved ones.

We were all attempting to heal from catastrophic situations. The strength in my legs and arms was slow to return. My balance was in worse shape. The first time on the parallel bars, learning to walk again was demoralizing. Even though I was secured in a harness for support, my legs felt useless. I would have crumpled to the ground without the safety it provided. My therapists urged me to push on, and I did, but the snaillike pace of learning to walk again was glacially slow.

On days when getting better seemed impossible, I wept. Then the memory of my father's words after I asked him how he had survived the Depression in 1929 as a 17-year-old, penniless, Irish immigrant with a sixth-grade education reverberated in my head.

"When you think you can't go on, you just put one foot in front of the other even if you don't know where you are going. If you fall, get up. The difference between survival and death is in not giving up. Never, ever quit," he'd say.

Day by day, it was hard to notice improvement, but week by week, I was definitely stronger. Finally, when I was strong enough to be brought to the main gym, I was helped into the wheelchair. With my wife and therapist, I propelled myself down the long corridor to the gym. I pushed the wheels on the wheelchair until my arms felt like they would fall off. My appreciation for wheelchair athletes grew immeasurably.

My first impression of the gym: it was breathtaking. The floor-to-ceiling windows soared over several stories with that same expansive view of the harbor. When the massive, fully loaded LNG tankers with their Coast Guard gun boats, tugboats, and helicopters guarding them came into view, it was impressive. (I noticed that when they left after unloading their cargo, they rode the waves much higher.)

Gazing around the enormous room, I watched patients, young and old, struggling to find their inner strength, to achieve their new normal. They were focused, and like me, struggled with the rigorous exercises. The physical therapists and occupational therapists continued to motivate us, pushing us to our limits and beyond. Push harder! You've got this! Words of encouragement and acknowledgment of everyone's effort were embedded in the Spaulding Hospital's rehabilitation culture. As I improved, the exercises got harder, much harder, but the team would not allow me to let up or quit.

My wheelchair was given to a new patient who needed it more than I did. Honestly, I was afraid to give up the apparatus that had given me newfound mobility. Now I had to learn to walk with "Lofstrand" crutches—just like the ones Forrest Gump used. These were specialized crutches designed for use by patients with neuromuscular problems. They were a bit awkward and hard to master. Embarrassment washed over me; I wanted the wheelchair back. I felt silly about wishing I could still use it, but it was so easy. Yet progress had to be encouraged, and each day I walked longer and longer distances with the new crutches.

As my arm and leg strength improved, physical therapy worked next on my flagging progress with balance. First, we used the balance bars, then a BOSU ball, which looks like a large rubber ball cut in half with wood covering the flat part. It's flipped over, and I had to learn to stand on the hard flat surface, keep my balance, and attempt to remain upright while the soft, rounded part wiggled away. This was the toughest exercise I had to do. It was much harder than it looked and the one exercise I truly dreaded and never fully mastered. My sense of balance was seriously impaired and would be the last issue to show improvement.

The therapists knew from experience that they needed multiple ways to challenge and motivate their patients and prevent boredom. One of the more interesting ways was using Nintendo Wii. To my chagrin, this was not just a child's game but a formidable exercise with clever feedback on whether you did the exercises correctly or not. I found that it really helped me and I enjoyed it!

Occupational therapists had designed a specific rehabilitation program for me. It focused on restoring independent personal care. I had to relearn how to get myself out of bed without assistance, shower, shave, and dress myself without falling. All things learned decades ago that I had taken for granted. One exercise had me washing, drying, and folding clothes, then bringing them back to my room in a laundry basket. Each task had to be mastered and got me one step closer to home. Madeline, my occupational therapist, had a dry sense of humor. One morning, she took me to the kitchen and had me make her scrambled eggs and toast, which she enjoyed. Next, I had to bake her brownies.

Sampling them, my wife had a good laugh. "Hey, he never made me brownies!" she joked.

For Valentine's Day, I was taken to art therapy where I was instructed to make a card for my wife. The last memory that I had of making a card was in elementary school or perhaps kindergarten. This task required more dexterity than I imagined. I was again humbled regarding how hard it was to be a patient.

One day, after it was felt that I had made enough progress, I was given a day pass. Colleen and I went out for lunch at our favorite restaurant on the Boston Harbor waterfront. I was shocked at how much strength it took out of me. Though exhausting, it had the desired effect and recharged my emotional batteries immeasurably. It was early March, and on good days, my wife or siblings would take me out for walks around the hospital grounds. These outings gave me hope that I would soon be released, but I first needed to prove that I could do so safely. The thought of going home was intoxicating. I convinced myself that I would be discharged within a week.

It was then that I fell victim to "The Stockdale Paradox," described by James Collins in his book *Good to Great*. Admiral Stockdale was a POW in Vietnam and spent eight years in the "Hanoi Hilton" where he was frequently tortured and placed in solitary confinement for months at a time. He noted that it was not the torture that broke soldiers but the solitary confinement. Prisoners who had a release date from captivity locked into their minds, which then came and went, became despondent and withered.

After being freed by the Viet Cong and arriving home, Stockdale was asked how he was able to not only survive but remain sane. He commented, "I never doubted that I would not only get out, but also that I would prevail in the end and turn the experience into the defining event of my life, which, in retrospect, I would not trade."

He was later asked, "Who didn't make it out?"

He replied, "The optimists. Oh, they were the ones who said, 'We're going to be out by Christmas.' And Christmas would come, and Christmas would go. Then they'd say, 'We're going to be out by Easter.' And Easter would come, and Easter would go. And then Thanksgiving, and then it would be Christmas again. And they died of a broken heart. This is a very important lesson. You must never confuse faith that you would prevail in the end—which you can never afford to lose—with the discipline to confront the most brutal facts of your current reality, whatever they might be."

Viktor Frankl had a similar observation from his experience as a prisoner in Auschwitz. Optimistic prisoners who mentally locked onto dates of release declined and died when the dates came and went.

When the day that I had picked in my head for going home from Spaulding Hospital came and went, the brutal facts became my reality. Up to that point, I had rarely cried, but this left me devastated, and I sobbed like a baby. I had made the mistake that Admiral Stockdale and Viktor Frankl had warned of. I hit a wall. As hard as I tried, I was stuck.

Someone thought that a visit from a therapy dog would help. It would have except that I was still on infection precautions and could not hold or even pet the dog. This was crushing. The dog sat quietly at my doorway with me looking at him. Someone later commented, "Let no good deed go unpunished." The silent dark void grew more powerful.

After a while, once again, my father's words played over and over inside my head. "Never ever quit. If you fall down, pick yourself up." I picked myself up emotionally and redoubled my efforts to get stronger with every ounce of determination I had in me. Just as Dr. Frankl advised, I identified a purpose in life and used my wife's strength and love to work beyond what I thought I was capable of doing. And of note is the inspiration that the physical structure of the Spaulding Hospital gym conveys, which is hard to describe. Although designed by gifted architects, it was the input of changes suggested by former patients that created the awe that inspires one to "Find Your Strength."

Learning to walk with crutches, to swallow, to shower and dress myself, was agonizingly slow and painful. The next challenges were harder still but essential to my being allowed to go home. Spaulding recognized the importance of spiritual and psychological healing in the rehabilitation process. This was included in the recovery plan of each patient. Goals were individualized, and achievement of these goals didn't always progress in a straight line.

One of my physical therapists came up with a creative plan to help me get past my latest setback. She had a passion for ballroom dancing, which she did competitively. My wife had mentioned that she loved to watch *Dancing with the Stars*, and one afternoon, my therapist surprised us with the exercise plan for the day: to practice ballroom dancing. The music started; Colleen's smile lit up the huge gym. We held hands, and my therapist talked us through our dance moves. It was a magical and joyful experience that made me feel alive despite the fact that I was a terrible dancer even when I was healthy. I was no Fred Astaire, but in my mind, it felt as though Colleen and I were really "Dancing with the Stars." My physical therapist had found one small thing that made all the difference.

As I grew stronger, I had more visitors. One afternoon, my best friend, Steve, and his wife, Carol, came to the hospital. Our children were the same age and grew up together, sailing in the ocean off Cape Cod in the summer and skiing in the winter. We had become a second set of parents to each other's children. Seeing them made me feel elated. They brought things to read and handed me a small bag with a candle from the replica of the Shrine to Our Lady of Lourdes from the campus of Notre Dame. The rosary is said there every day by a group of students and clergy. I had never been to Lourdes but had visited that Notre Dame Shrine with Steve and his family when my son Michael was looking at prospective colleges. His daughter, Laura, was enrolled as a freshman at the time. We stayed at a nearby bed and breakfast, spent too much money in the bookstore, and watched the Naval Academy football team fall to Notre Dame in the stadium known as the "House that Knute Rockne (ND's head coach) built."

"On the night you were taken to the Brigham and Women's Hospital, near death, Caroline and her husband Jason called Notre Dame. They asked that the students of Notre Dame say the rosary for you at the grotto," Steve said.

I stared into his eyes. It took me a few moments for the words to sink in, then I asked him to repeat what he had just said. It was in that instant that I realized the image of the woman in the luminous, shimmering robe that I had seen as I lay near death in the ICU was Our Lady of Lourdes. For the first time, I shared the memory of what had happened in the ICU at BWH. Until that moment I had never mentioned it. I told them I didn't know if I had hallucinated it or if I had really been dead, but the raw emotion of the memory of what I saw and heard came flooding back.

My hospital room became very quiet. No one said a word for some time until Carol said, "This was a true 'God Wink.'"

The power of prayer has always been a topic for speculation and differences of opinion, as not all prayers are answered. But at this moment, the power of prayer was apparent to not only me but to everyone in that room. I vowed two things. The first vow was that the day I was strong enough to travel to France, I would make a pilgrimage to the little town that is home to the Shrine of Our Lady of Lourdes. The second vow was to return to the University of Notre Dame and say thank you for the prayers.

Little by little, the team at Spaulding Hospital rebuilt me physically and emotionally. Although I had no idea if my life would ever come close to being what it was, I believed more steadfastly than ever in the immigrant's dream: anything is possible, though not guaranteed, as long as you imagine it and work hard to achieve it. My focus was simple: going home to my wife and resuming the practice of medicine.

Chapter 5

How Could This Happen? Understanding Viruses and Battling Against the Odds

"No one is so brave that he is not disturbed by something unexpected."
Julius Caesar

I kept asking myself over and over, how could this have happened? How was this possible? Every year I got my flu shot. I was up to date on my pneumococcal pneumonia vaccination. The importance of hand washing had been drilled into me since medical school, and I was very careful. It had become a reflex. I suppose I could have let my guard down, but the most likely scenario was that I fell victim to an airborne viral respiratory infection. These viruses are common and seasonal, waning in warm weather and flourishing in cold. December, when I became ill, was smack in the middle of the season.

Estimates suggest that over one-half billion non-influenza viral respiratory infections occur annually, making this the most common acute illness in the developed world. On average, adults get two to three viral infections each year. More than 200 different viruses cause the common cold, with the most frequent being rhinoviruses at 30 to 50 percent, followed by coronaviruses at 10 to 15 percent. Influenza virus causes approximately 5 to 15 percent of these infections with respiratory syncytial virus (RSV) and parainfluenza causing around 5 percent.[1,2,3] Typically, symptoms last from two to fourteen days and are self-limited—meaning no medical treatment is needed to recover. Rest, fluids, acetaminophen, as well as over-the-counter nonsteroidal medication, such as Ibuprofen, help relieve symptoms of fever and muscle ache. Antibiotics do not help in the treatment of viral illnesses, and their inappropriate use can predispose one to more serious infections or complications.

Respiratory viruses predominantly spread two ways: directly—through sneezing, coughing, talking, or by hand-to-face contact with an infected person; or indirectly (uncommon), following contact with an infected surface. Viruses can spread by both large and small particle aerosols released by breathing.[4] Studies have shown that we touch our faces 23 times an hour.[5] Handwashing with soap and water or alcohol-based hand sanitizer for 20 seconds kills viruses. The use of surgical masks is effective in preventing the transmission of both particle and droplet viruses. Simple measures work very well. Preventing an infection is much easier than hoping to survive one, or worse, enduring one of its more serious, even lethal, complications. Early on in the pandemic, health care providers who scrupulously followed these guidelines by using N95 masks and washing their hands

---

[1] G.L. Kirkpatrick, "The Common Cold," *Primary Care* 23, no.4 (December 1996): 657.

[2] Tehro Heikkinen and Asko Järvinen, "The Common Cold," *The Lancet* 361, no. 9351 (2003): 51.

[3] Ron Eccles, "Understanding the Symptoms of the Common Cold and Influenza," *The Lancet Infectious Diseases* 5, no.11 (2005): 718.

[4] R. B. Turner, "Epidemiology, Pathogenesis and the Treatment of the Common Cold," *Annals of Allergy, Asthma & Immunology* 78, no.6 (June 1997): 531.

[5] Yen Lee Angela Kwok, Jan Gralton, and Mary-Louise McLaws, "Face Touching: A Frequent Habit That Has Implications for Hand Hygiene," *American Journal of Infection Control* 43, no.2 (February 2015): 112-114.

before entering the rooms of patients stricken with COVID-19 had an extremely low likelihood of becoming infected.

Here's the history for how this knowledge made its way to modern times. During the Crimean war of 1853, Florence Nightingale was asked by the British government to organize a corps of nurses to care for the wounded soldiers at Scutari in Constantinople. Her practice of handwashing with soap and water, sanitation, and hygiene while caring for these soldiers led to a remarkable two-thirds decrease in death related to infection. Her results were transformative and rapidly changed the treatment of soldiers injured in war. These lessons were carried on in the nursing school that she later established. Florence Nightingale is considered the founder of modern nursing.[6]

In 1857, Louis Pasteur was the first scientist to prove the germ theory of illness, thereby disproving what, at the time, was the universal belief that infection was caused by spontaneous generation.[7] His discovery of pasteurization to eradicate pathogenic microorganisms found in raw milk and milk products (that otherwise could cause disease) remains in use today. Ten years later, Dr. Joseph Lister proved the value of handwashing with an antiseptic solution to prevent infection as postulated in Louis Pasteur's germ theory. In an article published in *The Lancet* in 1867, Dr. Lister introduced the revolutionary concept of using carbolic acid as an antiseptic in surgery to kill germs *before* they caused infection.[8] His innovation of handwashing with carbolic acid and his invention of applying carbolic acid to wounds via a spray can (as well as to surgical implements and dressings) led to a reduction in post-

---

[6] A. Ralby, "The Crimean War 1853 – 1856," *Atlas of Military History* (Parragon: 2013).

[7] Louis Pasteur, "Memoire sur la Fermentation Appele e Lactique," Comptes Rendu Hebdomadaires des Seances de l'Academie des Sciences 45 (1857): 913-916.

[8] J. Lister, "On a New Method of Treating Compound Fractures, Abscess, etc.," *The Lancet*, no. 2291 (1867): 91-120.

operative infections and revolutionized the practice of surgery. Amputation in that era was a common complication for patients with a compound fracture. Amputations plummeted with his antiseptic technique. British and American surgeons initially resisted the idea, but by 1875, a full eight years after his publication, handwashing and sterilization of instruments were widely adopted with countless lives and limbs saved. For this, Dr. Lister is regarded as the "Father of Surgery."

Even in retrospect, it is shocking to remember that the routine of universal precautions didn't start until well into the AIDS pandemic. During the late 1970s and early 1980s when I trained to be a physician, this was not the norm. Look at any rerun of an ER show from this era to get a sense of how much has changed. It took over 100 years and the tragedy of AIDS for the concept and practice of universal precautions to gain traction. Currently, medical and nursing personnel are scrupulous when washing their hands and use masks, gloves, and other personal protective equipment (PPE) to prevent transmission of all pathogens as an essential part of their day-to-day jobs.

Of note is the further expansion of disease prevention reflected in the award of the 1901 Nobel Prize in Medicine or Physiology to Emil von Behring for the scientific discovery of the importance of antibodies, serum, and vaccines in fighting infection. This proved especially successful in its application against diphtheria.[9]

Yet, viruses maintain a ferocity which eludes medicine's control over them, and the vulnerable remain. Elderly patients; those with lowered immunity from concomitant illnesses (including cancer); those who use medications that impair the immune system; or those who have pre-existing conditions (such as lung disease or diabetes) are more prone to all infections and their complications. Impaired sleep, poor

---

[9] 1901 Nobel Prize in Physiology (Medicine), Emil von Behring.

nutrition, and increased life stress lower immunity and make you more susceptible to illness by increasing cortisol levels. While regular exercise stimulates the immune system (as does adequate sleep and nutrition), older adults have been shown to have a typical age-related decrease in their immune function.

Several factors compromised my own health. Pain from my hip and back had prevented regular exercise for many months prior to my getting sick, thus depriving me of that boost in immunity. The combination of the winter viral season, being rundown from working long hours, and sleep deprivation due to waking up with physical pain made me a sitting duck for any illness. Ironically, my elective hip replacement surgery was scheduled for the week after I was admitted with pneumonia. In retrospect, I had failed to abide by my own maxim of the three A's: "Acknowledge (the facts of your situation), Accept (as denial will prevent you from moving forward), and Adapt (find an alternative path)," that I exhorted my patients to follow. I thought that I could just "gut it out" and power through my illness. It was hard for me to accept the needed hip replacement surgery, so I put it off for too long.

Over the years, I had witnessed first-hand the myriad negative outcomes that resulted from others who overextended themselves. Most people believe that they are twenty years younger than they really are, as strong as ever, and overestimate what they can manage. In youth, this trick of the mind helps you push beyond limits, past your fear, to reach your full potential. However, beginning in your fifth decade, this line of thought can get a person into trouble. Mine is a cautionary tale of thinking that somehow, I was invincible, that there would be no consequences of "burning the candle at both ends." It was true until the day it wasn't. I had made the same error and suffered the consequence of hubris or pride, a painful life lesson that ancient philosophers warned against.

It started with a dry, nagging cough and nothing else. A few days later, I felt fatigued. Vacation awaited me once I made it to the weekend. However, a low-grade fever was next, followed by shortness of breath and congestion. My physician ordered antibiotics and an inhaler when I started to wheeze and produce sputum. After several days, I was worse despite treatment. This prompted another visit to the doctor and an X-ray that revealed a small area of pneumonia, but the fever had abated, with a normal blood oxygen level and lab work. There was no indication for hospitalization, and I was sent home for the course of treatment to take effect. It was New Year's Eve 2013 when my wife was awakened by my labored breathing. She phoned 911 immediately.

Nasal congestion, nasal discharge, sore throat, muscle aches, and a general feeling of being unwell are frequent symptoms of a viral infection due to the body's immune response. Most common colds do not develop into anything serious, such as pneumonia, but viral respiratory infections can lead to community acquired pneumonia (CAP), which in the U.S. is the second most common cause of hospitalization after childbirth. However, pneumonia is the most common infectious cause of death. There are approximately 1,500,000 unique hospitalizations for CAP in the U.S. each year. Viruses are more common than bacteria as the cause of pneumonia requiring hospitalization. Rhinovirus is the most commonly detected virus among patients with CAP. Influenza was found to be the second most common etiology of pneumonia requiring hospitalization.[10,11,12]

---

[10] American Thoracic Society, "Top 20 Pneumonia Facts—2019," accessed June 13, 2024, https://www.thoracic.org/patients/patient-resources/resources/top-pneumoniafacts.pdf.

[11] Jennie Johnston, Sumit R. Majumdar, Julie D. Fox, and Thomas J. Marie, "Viral Infection in Adults Hospitalized with Community Acquired Pneumonia: Prevalence, Pathogens and Presentation," *Chest* 134, no.6 (December 2008): 1141-8.

[12] J. A. Ramirez, UpToDate, "Overview of Community Acquired Pneumonia in Adults," March 13, 2020.

Community acquired pneumonia (CAP), at 40 percent, is the most common cause of acute respiratory distress syndrome (ARDS), however ARDS is an uncommon complication of CAP. Surprisingly, 62 percent of adult patients requiring hospitalization to treat pneumonia have no identifiable cause of their pneumonia found.[13] The path a virus may travel to arrive at what happened to me—ARDS—is as follows: After entrance of viral pathogens, they colonize the nasopharynx. When the virus next reaches the lungs, it continues to replicate there. The body's immune response leads to inflammation and damage to the lung tissue, resulting in pneumonia. This immune response in the smallest part of the lungs (alveoli) plays an important role in determining the severity of the disease. For some patients, there is a well-contained, local inflammatory response. Less commonly, a systemic response is triggered in order to control the infection. In rare cases, this systemic immune response can become uncontrolled, leading to severe lung damage, overwhelming infection (sepsis), and respiratory failure—ARDS. And as I've written, relating my own experience, this condition requires life support with intubation and mechanical ventilation. The body's own immune protective mechanism becomes uncontrolled and runs amok, causing indiscriminate damage to the body it's supposed to protect, resulting in potential organ failure and even death.

So, what was I dealing with? ARDS was first described during the Vietnam War when military clinicians working in surgical hospitals noted a distinct type of respiratory failure. It was characterized by an acute abnormality of both lungs, and they named it shock lung.[14] On a normal chest X-ray, healthy

---

[13] M.D. Siegel, UpToDate, "Acute Respiratory Distress Syndrome: Prognosis and Outcomes in Adults," March 6, 2017.

[14] D. G. Ashbaugh, D. B. Bigelow, T. L. Petty, and B. E. Levine, "Acute Respiratory Distress in Adults." *The Lancet* 2, no. 7511. (August 1967): 319.

lungs appear black, signifying air is where it should be, with the white of the bones and heart shadow indicating density greater than air. With pneumonia, usually one segment or one subsegment of the lung appears white, representing fluid and debris from the pneumonia. With ARDS, all segments of both lungs show only white. The term "bilateral white out" is used to describe the chest X-ray appearance indicating that all segments of the lung are compromised by this process. This can occur in children as well as adults. Thirty percent are classified as mild, 47 percent as moderate, and 23 percent as severe. The mortality for ARDS is 35 percent when mild, 40 percent when moderate, and over 46 percent when severe. In the elderly, mortality for ARDS is up to 58 percent.[15, 16] My diagnosis was severe ARDS with perhaps a 50 percent or less chance of survival.

Normal lung function requires a dry surface with the smallest balloon-like, air-filled sacs (alveoli) to be open (patent) and in close contact with the smallest blood vessels (capillaries) for oxygen to be efficiently transferred from the lung into the blood. I was taught as an intern that "a dry lung is a happy lung." However, in ARDS (in essence, an inflammatory condition), the injury to the alveoli causes release of pro-inflammatory cytokines. These then recruit the killing component of white blood cells (neutrophils) to the lungs to fight the infection. They become activated and release toxic mediators that damage the critical junction between the capillary and alveoli, releasing protein-rich fluid that fills the lungs, impeding the transfer of oxygen from the lungs into the blood stream. This increase in fluid within the lungs combined with the damage to the

---

[15] G. Bellani et al., "Epidemiology, Patterns of Care, and Mortality for Patients with Acute Respiratory Distress Syndrome in Intensive Care Units in 50 Countries," *JAMA* 315, vol.8 (February 2016): 788-800.

[16] Chen Y. Wang et al., "One-Year Mortality and Predictors of Death Among Hospital Survivors of Acute Respiratory Distress Syndrome," *Intensive Care Medicine* 40, no. 3 (March 2014): 388-96.

smallest part of the lung tissue causes the airspace to fill with edema fluid and debris from the degenerating cells. The alveoli then collapse. This is the "unhappy lung" that I was taught how to care for during my medical residency training.

There is neither a cure nor an effective medication to treat ARDS. As I've described, my own care was supportive: intubation, mechanical ventilation to force oxygen under pressure into the fluid-filled lungs, nutrition, and the prevention of blood clots and gastrointestinal ulcers along with other potentially life-threatening complications. Since intubation and mechanical ventilation is extremely unpleasant when fully awake, patients are typically given a combination of benzodiazepines and opioids to relieve anxiety and pain. Muscular paralysis with curare-like medications (Nimbex Cisatracurium besylate or similar medications) improves tolerance of mechanical ventilation and decreases oxygen requirements. These curare-like medications can cause prolonged neuromuscular weakness. High-dose steroids (dexamethasone) may be given to patients with moderate to severe ARDS due to CAP who have evidence of a life-threatening or dysregulated immune response to the infection, but steroids also have potentially serious complications.[17]

I was fortunate to achieve adequate oxygen levels with mechanical ventilation. Patients who don't can be placed on an artificial lung known as extracorporeal membrane oxygenation (ECMO). This heroic procedure entails placing large catheters into blood vessels in the neck and leg. The patient's blood is then passed through a specialized machine that takes over the lung's function. The blood bypasses the damaged lungs and moves through the ECMO machine, thereby transferring life-

---

[17] A. Artigas et al., "The American-European Consensus Conference on ARDS, Part 2. Ventilatory, Pharmacologic, Supportive Therapy, Study Design Strategies and Issues Related to Recovery and Remodeling. Acute Respiratory Distress Syndrome." *American Journal of Respiratory and Critical Care Medicine* 157, no.4 pt. 1 (April 1998): 1332-47.

sustaining oxygen into the blood, which is then pumped back into the body to keep the organs alive. This is a high-risk, last-ditch effort that even if it succeeds can lead to serious adverse outcomes such as stroke. This procedure is only available in some of the highly specialized, academic, tertiary medical centers and is why I was transferred to Brigham and Women's Hospital.

I did require high-dose steroids to treat my ARDS. Steroids have a powerful but non-selective ability to suppress the dys-regulated immune response but with many adverse side effects. Corticosteroids are truly double-edged sword medications, or as I was taught in medical school, "poisons with desirable side effects." Current recommendations are to reserve steroids for pa-tients with moderate to severe ARDS who have evidence of an uncontrolled immune response to the viral illness. I was placed on high-dose intravenous steroids for a very long time, and al-though they indisputably helped save my life, the complications which I was to later experience nearly resulted in my death. High-dose dexamethasone has become the standard of care for moderate to severe ARDS caused by COVID-19 to treat the hyper-immune response now known as a cytokine storm.

If you survive ARDS, what can happen next may be even harder to recover from. Rates of cognitive dysfunction following ARDS vary among studies, ranging from 25 to 78 percent. Psychiatric illnesses also appear to be common among survivors, with depression, anxiety, and post-traumatic stress disorder as the most regularly reported. Family members of ARDS survivors can also struggle with these issues. Frequently, persistent, abnormal exercise endurance and physical disabilities remain. Lung function following ARDS is often compromised for as long as five years after the acute illness.[18]

---

[18] M. E. Mikkelsen, G. Netzer, and T. Iwashyna, UpToDate, "Post-Intensive Care Syndrome," October 4, 2015.

Enduring and surviving ARDS differs from recovery and resuming your life. Somehow, I beat the odds of not only surviving and escaping the most feared complications, but in resuming my life as a physician. It is unknown how intensive rehabilitation impacts these complications in survivors of ARDS, as many are sent off to nursing homes or long-term acute care facilities (LTACs), where there is little long-term outcome data. However, it has been shown that patients who participate in specialized, structured rehabilitation—whether following cardiac incidents, stroke, spinal cord trauma, or joint replacement procedures—all achieve a better functional status than patients who do not. It seems logical that this strategy will yield positive results in other rehabilitation scenarios such as survivors of COVID-19 ARDS.

And although I've no proof, I strongly feel that the reason I did not fall victim to the gruesome statistics cited above is due to the 24/7 support of my family, the outstanding pulmonary critical care team at BWH, and the intense, structured therapy at Spaulding Hospital. The rehabilitation phase of my healing journey (both inpatient and outpatient) was not without setbacks and detours. It lasted much longer than the initial acute illness and is why specialized rehabilitation is so critical to achieving your full recovery potential. I owe my life to the physicians and nurses at Brigham and Women's Hospital, but I owe my recovery to the physical, occupational, and speech therapists at Spaulding Hospital.

Chapter 6

Jesuit Education

*"Education is the most powerful weapon
which you can use to change the world."*
Nelson Mandela

I n my search for guidance on how to survive and recover from
a life-altering, near-to-death experience, I found that no one
had all the answers. There is no guidebook. My reading made
it clear that it is a uniquely different experience for everyone,
but common themes emerged. Never quit. Endure. Survive. My
Jesuit education, as well as reading throughout life, exposed me
to stories of people who went through unimaginable suffering
yet went on to lead productive lives full of love. The totality of
these survivor accounts and how they found the strength to not
only come out the other end from their trauma but to overcome
their life challenges spoke to me. These were not broken people
nor were they simply lucky survivors who beat the odds. They
seemed to truly become better people *because* of their life
experiences. I desperately wanted to join their ranks.

In retrospect, how I responded to the crucible of pain
that I went through was shaped by the humble yet profoundly
insightful teachings of my father and my eight years of Jesuit
education at Boston College High School (BCH) and Boston
College (BC). I found the observation attributed to Confucious
that, "The greatest glory in living lies not in ever falling, but

rising every time we fall," to be true and to echo the lessons taught by my father.

Books by ancient Greek philosophers, theologians, the psychiatrist Viktor Frankl, Admiral James Stockdale, and others that I had previously read, now resonated in a different way. What I had been taught during my education became integrated at a more personal level. The irony is that it took over four decades to fully appreciate what I had learned. We entered BCH and BC as boys who then graduated as men with a moral compass, and what I later realized were the foundational skills needed for life. Many lessons of the past were subliminal, gained by exposure to courses on the classics, philosophy, theology and history. (Which I strongly encourage everyone to study!) They lodged deep inside as memories undetected and unappreciated until the time when I needed them. Then they were invaluable.

As a fourteen-year-old boy and later as an eighteen-year-old college freshman, classes on those subjects seemed to be not only superfluous but onerous. I wanted to study science but I was drawn to them. The Cold War was growing in intensity. President John F. Kennedy audaciously challenged Americans to be the first to land a man on the moon. At that time, America was losing the space race to Russia. It became almost a patriotic duty to master science. It was science that helped save my life but it was my exposure to ancient Greek philosophers and to history that was critical to my enduring, processing, and recovering from what was otherwise an impossible experience to prepare for.

Words are powerful. With each life experience, words take on a more individual significance. In elementary school, spelling was my first introduction to words. Education in Boston during the 1960s and 1970s was rigid and didactic. Each morning we said the Pledge of Allegiance with our right hand over our hearts. This was followed by the "Duck and Cover Drill," where we huddled under our desks for protection in case of a nuclear bomb explosion, courtesy of the Cuban Missile Crisis. After spelling drills, we lined up around the walls of the classroom. Your name was called, and you were quizzed on the words. If you made a mistake, you had to sit down—humiliating. As a child, I understood the meaning of the words: "fear" (scared) and "terror" (wicked scared). Over the years these two words gained greater context. Following the assassination of President Kennedy, a deeper, more granular understanding of their meaning took root. Following my being near death, my fight for survival, and the arduous recovery that ensued, my understanding of these words profoundly changed.

A particular story that had made an outsized impact on me and then supported an aspect of my psychological healing, was that of Admiral James Stockdale. He credits his knowledge of philosophy, garnered as a graduate student at Stanford, in unknowingly preparing him for his eight years as a POW in Vietnam. He learned intimately that, "We are all our brother's keeper."

He taught other POWs how to emotionally and physically survive, despite relentless brutality and privation. Under the hands of skilled North Vietnamese torturers, every POW broke, thus violating the Military Code of Conduct. The subsequent shame was shattering for these officers, many who were graduates of the Naval Academy. Stockdale gained awareness that the guilt that resulted from "spilling your guts" under torture was what broke the prisoners, not the torture itself. He realized that the guards wanted to emotionally break them and use them as propaganda puppets. He knew he could not stop other prisoners, or even himself, from saying things under torture that they would regret. Stockdale devised a post-torture debriefing where each man told the other prisoners what they had admitted to, then the group would absolve them of guilt. Confession was truly sanity saving for many of these men. At the end of the war, when all were released, Admiral Stockdale found that his men suffered far less emotional and psychological damage than those who did not follow his lead.

In the words of Epictetus, his favorite Greek philosopher: "Difficulties are what show men's character."

This theme of guilt, and overcoming it, ran through many of the stories of survival that I read. Survivor guilt is a common experience in those who do not succumb to illness, natural disasters, death camps, and in soldiers who experience combat. This guilt was something that I never fully understood or experienced until later in my recovery when I was home. Word reached me that a colleague had died of an illness. He was many years younger than I and a father with small children. This seemed so unfair! Why did I live and not him? I could not shake this feeling.

Later, this nagging sense of guilt grew. Thoughts clouded my thinking: If I had done more to maintain my health, this illness would not have happened. I felt shame that I was the cause of so much emotional pain for my wife and family. Gradually, I came to realize that this guilt was a trap that anyone could easily fall prey to. No one is in control of random life events. Guilt and anger are useless emotions that impede recovery. Self-compassion and forgiveness are essential to resiliency and healthy recovery. Forgiveness of self and others is crucial to healing from any trauma. Admiral Stockdale's insight into guilt and the power of forgiveness was transformational. He was later awarded the Congressional Medal of Honor for his leadership.

In a speech years later, Admiral Stockdale stated, "The challenge of education is not to prepare people for success but for failure." Business school studies have shown that the most powerful lessons are learned from failed businesses. It is rare to find a thriving business venture that is led by people who have never experienced failure. This narrative gives further credence to what Aristotle observed: "Education is ornamental in good times and essential in bad times." I have found this to be true.

When I look back to discover what led me to a career in medicine, I must credit my Jesuit Education. Its academic framework, the "Ratio Studiorum," encourages students to be guided by principles of ethical living, service to others, the search for truth, and a passion for justice. The rubric we learned under was "JUG," aka justice under God. The importance of altruism was introduced with the tradition of the MITE Box. This is credited to Reverend Henry J. Wessling, SJ, who in 1924, organized a weekly collection to raise money to alleviate suffering wherever it existed. It took me many years to fully appreciate the value of philanthropy and altruism. The greatest value accrues not to the person receiving but to the person giving. At its core, selfless giving is one of the fundamental keys to happiness. "What counts in life is not the mere fact that we have lived. It is the difference we have made to the lives of others that will determine the significance of the life we lead," said Nelson Mandela.

We were also taught the concept of individual responsibility as well as accountability, not only for our words but for our actions. Little by little our moral compass was developed as was our resiliency. I had to dig deep to regain my health and rebuild my life. The ability to push myself to my limits and beyond had been instilled in me by my demanding Jesuit educators.

We were graded on effort as well as performance. The fact that the most successful individuals in life often were not the smartest or most gifted but the hardest working was constantly repeated. You do not have to be the school valedictorian or team captain to be successful. (This was a good thing, as I was never number one or captain of anything but I excelled at hard work.) We were taught that good habits are a powerful force in life. They are hard to make, and conversely, bad habits are even harder to break. Habits tend to be self-reinforcing. The best teachers and coaches work hard to instill a good work ethic. They know that practice teaches discipline and is essential for success at whatever you are trying to master. Consistent practice leads to a positive feedback loop, improved self-confidence, and the belief that hard work can overcome most obstacles in life. At home, my father's life exemplified what I learned in school regarding the value of respect for others, unwavering optimism, and hard work.

I am grateful that the belief in how essential it is to mentally as well as physically commit to the work needed to succeed became embedded in me when I was young. Science underpins this work ethic. Muscle memory comes from repetitive drilling whether it be math tables, reciting a poem, playing a musical instrument or a sport. It is important to understand that muscle memory is not solely about the muscle but rather the memory formed in the brain. Neural plasticity, a truly amazing biological process, is the ability of the brain to make new memories and develop new skills. Although most learning happens as children and adolescents, brains at any age have the capacity to do so. The brain tells the muscles what to do. The more we practice, the stronger the memory becomes, to the point when the skill becomes almost reflexive. You no longer need to think about what happens. It flows. It's been estimated that it takes about three thousand hours of practice (one or two hours a day, six days a week for five years), to become very good at what you are trying to do. It takes approximately ten thousand hours over ten years to attain mastery. In addition, a commitment to life-long practice and learning is required to maintain the skill; otherwise, the neural pathways that took years to develop atrophy.

So, while science offered the possibility of my body recovering, life skills embedded in me by my father and my Jesuit education were essential for my healing. They were the remedy when fear and terror overwhelmed me as I found myself having to relearn all that had been lost: the ability to breathe, swallow, walk, and return to my career as a physician. They offered hope that unrelenting effort can overcome adversity. Again, the words of Nelson Mandela rang true: "Courage is not the absence of fear, but the triumph over it."

Chapter 7

The Long Road

"It does not matter how slowly you go as long as you do not stop."
Confucius

I n order to return home, I had to meet Spaulding Hospital's criteria for a *safe* discharge. This meant proving that I could get out of bed, bathe, feed, and dress myself without assistance. These tasks were doable, although they took me several hours to accomplish. By far, the final test was the hardest: I had to get myself up from where I lay on the floor, flat on my back like an upside-down turtle, to a standing position—without using a device or receiving any help. This sequence of motion required numerous muscles to be strong and coordinated. This box took the longest to check.

By March 2014, I was discharged and thus began the longest leg of my recovery. The first goal had been to get home to my wife alive, and I had achieved it. The second goal was to return to the care of my patients, but this seemed to be, at best, uncertain. Just about everyone wanted me to retire. No one believed I could return to what I had been doing before my illness. Deep down, no matter how irrational this thought appeared, I maintained an unwavering belief in my ability to do whatever was needed, no matter how hard or how long it took, to return to medicine as a practicing physician. Even if my role as a physician had to change (which I began to accept), somehow, I would find a way to adapt, to improvise, to follow my father's Depression-era lesson to use what you *had*—not what you wanted or thought you needed to achieve your goal. Stories of others, who had not only survived but resumed meaningful lives despite suffering immense personal tragedy, were at the top of my mind and a constant companion.

Once home, the VNA provided nursing, physical and occupational therapy services, several days a week. The daily regimentation and intensity that I had at Spaulding Hospital was no longer present, and the outpatient therapies were boring. The biggest strides with any rehabilitation occur during the first months. Complete recovery is not guaranteed, and even when it's possible, it can take months to years. It was during this third phase of recovery that I began to understand why so many patients never met their full recovery potential. It quickly became clear that I had to structure my day with as much regimentation as I could. Otherwise, my exercise routine would become random, and I did not want to pay the consequences: loss of the strength and mobility I had worked so hard to attain.

Late winter 2014 was still too cold and slippery to walk safely outside. Fortunately, we had exercise equipment in the basement from when my sons were young. Although I had met the criteria for discharge, I was not strong enough to do what I had been capable of prior to ARDS. Even more humbling was that I wasn't strong enough to do what I had thought possible once I arrived home. The process was to be long, tedious, interrupted with setbacks, and overshadowed by an unknown future. One day, my wife silently hung the Serenity Prayer by Reinhold Niebuhr in our home.

> God grant me the serenity
> To accept the things I cannot change,
> The courage to change the things I can, and

The wisdom to know the difference

Later she hung up a favorite Dr. Seuss quote:

"You have brains in your head. You have feet in
your shoes.
You can steer yourself any direction you choose."

Upon discharge, I had been given a 1-inch binder of exercises, and the routine of morning and early afternoon exercise sessions at Spaulding Hospital was fresh in my mind. I replicated them as closely as possible. That was when my energy level was highest. My goal was to build on my body's current level of strength and flexibility. My fear was that I would lose what I had worked so hard to gain. I started an exercise journal to track: my tendon stretching; time on the exercise bike; core exercises; upper- and lower-body workouts. Fatigue exerted a constant drag on what I wanted to accomplish. For months I needed to nap at least once a day. Poor balance remained an impediment to using a treadmill. In the late afternoon and early evening, I read medical journals and did continuing medical education, using Audio Digest for Cardiology and Internal Medicine, including graded tests.

Boredom became one of the most difficult hurdles to overcome. Finding ways to keep myself motivated was an even bigger challenge. I kept a graph of my progress that measured my time and distance on the stationary bike. Each week I set my goal higher—even if it was only by adding a minute or one pushup. Over many months, I went from 5 minutes and not quite a quarter mile, to 60 minutes and 12 miles or more. Similarly, I kept track of how long I could hold a plank, how many abdominal crunches, bridges, and pushups I could do. Identifying how much weight I could lift and how many repetitions I could perform reminded me of high school, but at this age it was infinitely harder.

My progress was slow, very slow. As motivated as I was, as hard as I drove myself, recovery didn't match my expectations. The reality was that the therapists at Spaulding knew how to skillfully and carefully push me and the other patients past the limits created by fear. At home, I was afraid of hurting myself and suffering a setback. Fear was a constant companion. My life as I knew it was no more, and the contours of this new normal were unknown. Although improved, my lungs were significantly damaged, and I was still on home nocturnal oxygen. I could walk but not without a walker or crutches. I remained a fall risk due to compromised balance. I could not yet drive. Constant pain limited me since my hip replacement, set for January of 2014, had been cancelled and could not be rescheduled, as I was no longer a good surgical candidate.

One of the many lessons my father had taught me was that you can't change the cards you are dealt in life, but it's how you play those cards that matters. You have to be brutally honest with yourself at all times, never overestimate or underestimate the circumstances you find yourself in. The reality of my position was clear: my mind was strong, but my body was broken, albeit slowly mending. The time needed for my recovery and to what extent it was even possible was neither known nor guaranteed. Thank goodness that my wife and family were rocks that kept me from giving up and drifting away.

By the end of April 2014, I was working a few hours a week performing administrative duties. My home-exercise progress hit a wall, and I couldn't find a way to surmount it. With the month of May came warmer weather, and I was able to use my walker outside. Later in the month, I was allowed to start outpatient PT and OT. Thus began the third phase of my rehabilitation. The structure and supervision fostered confidence. I was able to increase my time on the exercise bike and I was assigned new exercises. Little by little, my upper-body, lower-body, and core strength increased. Office work expanded to eight hours a week but without patient contact.

In early June 2014, I had a setback requiring hospitalization. The endurance and muscle strength that I had worked so hard to regain withered away. Work was no longer possible nor was PT or OT. Three more hospitalizations and one more surgery created a roadblock on the route to recovery. Over the summer, I discovered the benefits of swimming. The lack of weight-bearing that swimming allowed helped me gain strength and endurance without being limited by my hip or back pain. Once again, I was strong enough to return to administrative work.

My orthopedic surgeon challenged me: if I could stay healthy and out of the hospital for three months, he would replace my hip. At my pre-op evaluation, I was advised to download a meditation by Peggy Huddleston from her book *Prepare for Surgery, Heal Faster: A Guide of Mind-Body Techniques*. It was designed to decrease pain following surgery. I was skeptical but complied.

October 10, 2014—my long-awaited left hip was finally replaced at Brigham Women's Hospital. In the recovery room, I was asked by one of the nurses to rate my pain.

I responded, "I have no pain."

The retort was, "You must have some pain."

I repeated, "I have no pain but do feel some minor discomfort at my incision site."

Their final response was, "You had good anesthesia."

At the time, it did not occur to me that the training in meditation from Peggy Huddleston had made a difference, but it had. Months later, my wife gave the tapes to a relative who had surgery scheduled, with similar results: minimal post-operative pain. Months later we compared notes regarding the meditation. We both acknowledged that the tapes had helped but could not explain why or how our pain was lessened.

Following the hip replacement, it was back to Spaulding Hospital for intense in-patient physical therapy. One of my therapists remarked, "Each day in the hospital requires one week of rehabilitation." Upon reflection, that seemed to match my experience.

By January 2015, I was allowed to drive. My hip pain was finally gone, but constant back pain limited walking or standing for very long; but I had achieved my second goal. I was allowed to return to patient care. This started as a significantly limited amount of time seeing patients. Little by little, I entered a virtuous cycle or a positive feedback loop of increased exercise and patient care. The stronger I became, the more I was able to do and the more I wanted to do. My strength and endurance grew.

Our son Patrick was living in Paris and working towards a master's degree at the Sorbonne. When I was intubated in the BWH ICU, one of the dream vacations I pledged to take my wife on was to Paris. I also wanted to keep the promise to make a pilgrimage to Lourdes. April 2015, we arrived in France. Patrick was our personal guide, and we were impressed with the detail of our itinerary that he had spent hours planning. We saw more than we thought possible, including all the highlights of Paris, Versailles, and Giverny. The Cathedral of Notre Dame was breathtaking. We went on an underground tour of the Catacombs of Paris, which the French Resistance had effectively used during World War II (not an activity for those who are claustrophobic).

Colleen and I had watched the movie *Saving Private Ryan* before our vacation. We booked a guided day trip with a trained historian to view the June 6, 1944, D-Day invasion site at Normandy. We read the history of Operation Overlord and D-Day itself. Our guide related, with powerful insight, the effects that both the German invasion and the Allied invasion had on French civilians. To actually be there was beyond amazing. It was like walking into history. Decades later, many German bunkers and the temporary port built for the invasion remained. The more than 9,000 headstones in the Normandy American Cemetery and Memorial bore solemn truth to the fact that the majority of those who died on the beaches of Normandy were boys, barely eighteen years old. The memorial to the 225 soldiers of the 2nd Battalion, 75th Ranger Regiment, who climbed the 100-foot cliffs of Pointe du Hoc, under withering attack, and the story of their heroism that day was profound. After two days of intense fighting, only 90 of the 225 Rangers survived. The selfless courage shown by so many was truly humbling. The ultimate sacrifice that these young men made in order for freedom to be restored and tyranny destroyed resonated in a way no history course or movie had ever reached me. What these men died for, yet again, exemplified that "We are all our brother's keeper."

I kept my promise to visit Lourdes. The flight was a short one from Paris to the Tarbes-Lourdes-Pyrenees Airport. The actual grotto was as I remembered in my mind's eye when I lay dying in the BWH ICU. Even now, it's hard to wrap my mind around the temporal connection between the prayers said for me by the students of Notre Dame, the memory of what I saw, and the sudden improvement in my breathing. Science cannot explain what happened, though I have sought an explanation. It can only be understood through faith—if you have it—otherwise, it is inexplicable. This connection to Notre Dame and my gratitude for what they did for me will remain forever. This trip was spiritually restorative, amazing in myriad ways, and recharged us both emotionally. Physically, however, the trip was demanding and exacted a heavy price.

May 10, 2015, I awoke with abdominal pain and was hospitalized once more: this time for acute diverticulitis, complicated by an abscess. Following prolonged intravenous antibiotics, on June 8, 2015, I underwent urgent surgery to remove the abscessed section of bowel. At first everything went well, then on June 13, 2015, my life was in jeopardy once more. I was re-hospitalized with an abdominal catastrophe; a rare surgical complication had occurred. Impaired healing was another complication from prolonged high-dose steroids. The sutures holding the repaired bowel together came apart. By the time I arrived in the emergency room at BWH, I was in septic shock, hypotensive, and near death for the second time. At some point, I lost consciousness. When I awoke, I knew where I was, and I remembered everything. This time it was the Brigham surgeons who saved my life.

The image of the woman in white floating above me had remained; it was still not my time to die. However, to almost die a second time imploded my world more profoundly than the first. After spending over a year enduring painful rehabilitation, I had returned to work as a physician caring for patients. My life had regained its meaning and purpose. Even though it was not the same, I was happy. Now, lying in bed, I felt as though I had been swallowed by a black hole in the universe with no way out. I didn't know whether I had the strength to go through the arduous, all-consuming but necessary effort of rebuilding my shredded and broken body again.

The abdominal catastrophe I had suffered was one of the most dreaded complications. It required an emergency ileostomy. My abdominal wall was left open, as the contaminated area could not be sutured together. The sensory overload that hit me when I first looked at the gaping abdominal wound caused my mind to go numb. Each time I tried to reason through what was happening, my thoughts acted like an accidental explosion of fireworks inside my head—random, unstructured, unrelated strands of words and emotions that made no sense. Although I had escaped death, this felt like too much to recover from. I could not envision how I could get back to even where I was just a few weeks ago, let alone what I had been steadily working towards for fifteen months. I knew that I couldn't quit, but I struggled with how to begin. Shock overwhelmed my family; this seemed too much to overcome. Job and I seemed to have too much in common. The fear that washed over me was at a deeper level than I had ever experienced.

My sister Maureen reached out to our friend and former neighbor Father Robert Keane, S.J., who happened to be a Jesuit priest. She asked him to come visit me in the hospital. He found me at my lowest point, overwhelmed and despondent. Somehow, his words reached me. I found the strength to once more travel on the path towards healing. This second near-death event came much closer to breaking me than the first. Again, I was reminded of how faith can often help you find a way when there does not appear to be a way or even a direction. A week later, I was discharged home, nearly, but not quite irrevocably, broken.

Giving up was never an option. Little by little, I discovered the inner strength to rebuild myself physically and emotionally. Progress crawled, as I was limited by the abdominal wound that the VNA had to pack regularly. The wound finally healed, and on August 26, 2015, my ileostomy was closed. My exercise and study routines improved. September 8, 2015, I returned to work part time, and by October 30, 2015, I was working in the office full time. However, my days of covering emergencies in the hospital were over.

Frederick Nietzsche famously said, "He who has a 'why' to live for can bear almost any 'how.'" When I look back on these events and try to understand how I got through it all, the inescapable answer of "how" was that I never lost sight of the "why": my wife, my life's purpose, and the realization that my life still had meaning. The memory of what I learned from my father, from the Jesuits, from Viktor Frankl, from James Stockdale, and so many others over the decades, along with my willingness to acknowledge, accept, adapt, to never quit, and to somehow find a way to overcome whatever obstacles I encountered, helped me find the way. What at the time seemed impossible was simply difficult.

Chapter 8

Pain

"Pain is something you carry, like a radio. You feel your strength in the experience of pain. It's all in how you carry it. That's what matters."
Jim Morrison

One day, my wife asked me to clean out my insanely cluttered nightstand. There were books and notepads covered with thoughts, observations, and goals, mixed up with plain old junk. Deep inside the drawer, I found the long-forgotten Peggy Huddleston meditation tape on reducing post-operative pain that I had successfully used prior to my hip replacement. It had been loaned out to others who also found the meditation tape helpful in diminishing pain following surgery. Since listening to it, I had done a great deal of reading on pain and had personally experienced a lot of good and bad days related to it. Pain had become a part of my daily life.

Estimates of pain are, at best, an inexact science and highly variable even among patients experiencing the same condition or pain-inducing stimulus. Unlike the quantifying of blood pressure, temperature, weight, or pulse rate, all of which yield measurable, reproducible data, grading pain on a scale of 0 to 10 is highly subjective. Pain fluctuates person to person and day to day. In fact, it's often a part of daily experience for people over age 50. True absence of pain only occurs with deep general anesthesia. As health care providers, alleviating pain and suffering is part of what we attempt to achieve for our patients. Its unpredictable nature creates quite the challenge to do so.

It is important to understand the differences between acute pain and chronic pain. Examples of acute pain include skin wounds and fractured bones. Skin wounds—even those that require sutures to close—can take one week to heal. Fractured bones can take six weeks, rarely longer, to heal. I was familiar with acute pain due to tissue damage and swelling. With healing, the pain lessens each day. Usually, acute pain requires no medication or at most, the brief use of over-the-counter agents with the need diminishing daily. The pain from being intubated was vastly worse than anything I had ever experienced, and it was unrelenting. This was acute pain; however, once the breathing tube was removed, the pain ceased.

Chronic pain usually lasts longer than six months, well beyond the time needed to heal. My chronic pain started insidiously. In 2012, the pain in my hip and back was more of a mild discomfort after working out on the treadmill or at the end of a long workday. As months passed, the discomfort transitioned to pain, which became more limiting. There was no one thing or defining event, only the steady erosion of my ability to carry out my job and the activities of daily living without pain. At work, I increasingly found myself needing to sit down and rest until it abated. Eventually, I was unable to walk or stand for very long because of the pain in my hip and back. By 2013, something as simple as rolling over while sleeping would jolt me awake with pain from my hip.

The dangers of too much acetaminophen (liver or hepatic toxicity), of non-steroidal anti-inflammatory medications (bleeding ulcers or kidney damage), and of opioid narcotics (constipation, nightmares, addiction) were well known, so I avoided them. After a tiring day, I placed ice packs on my lower back and hip. Multiple surgeries seemed to be the only reasonable option, but they would have to wait awhile longer.

Early in 2014, after surviving ARDS, I had been transferred from Brigham and Women's Hospital to Spaulding Hospital for inpatient physical therapy. At that point I became aware of how pain control was a fundamental part of every day and different for each patient. Now that I was off life support, the opioids I was given were not as powerful. Due to my hip and back pain, I was strongly encouraged to regularly take pain killers *before* my demanding physical therapy. The message was that the opioids would allow me to push harder and accomplish more on my road to recovery. Initially, this made sense. I would do whatever it took to help me get better, home to my wife, and to resume work. Every four hours I was asked to rate my pain on a scale from "0 to 10," followed by: Do you want one or two "Oxy"? Subtly, opioid pain medication became one with the rehabilitation process.

In patients predisposed to dependency, this problem can easily become more serious than the pain that opioids are supposed to relieve. This vulnerability can be uncovered using a simple screening assessment known as the "Opioid Risk Tool." I also learned of a second, much less common problem that some patients experience, termed "opioid-induced hyperalgesia (OIA)." The longer you take these medications, the more sensitive you can become to *any* painful stimuli, thus entering a vicious negative feedback loop. The part of your brain that registers pain erroneously tells you that you feel *more* pain, even if nothing has changed. Therefore, you feel the need for ever greater amounts of opioids.

Other side effects include "opioid-induced constipation," which in retrospect, contributed to the second time that I came inches from death. Constipation aggravated the age- and diet-related diverticulosis that had silently lurked inside of me. Additionally, the "Oxy" made my thinking feel foggy. I was not myself. The opioids fueled nightmares and seriously disturbed my sleep. Yet one or two Oxy had become the pre-physical therapy routine to allow maximal effort. This made sense until one day when I heard a new patient begin to plead, then scream as loud as he could, for his "Oxy" ahead of schedule. The chilling realization of how easily you could become dependent on opioids registered.

That moment of clarity made me decide to cut back on pain medication before I became dependent. I switched from two "Oxy" to one and only before the most rigorous physical therapy. Shortly thereafter, I refused to take them when offered.

One day, I asked the nurse, "Why do you ask patients to rate their pain every four hours?"

"Pain is the fifth vital sign," was the response.

Later, I asked one of the resident physicians caring for me about this.

"Adequate pain control is needed for the body to properly heal," she said.

This was puzzling. During medical school, residency, and fellowship training, I had been taught that treatment of acute pain is clearly indicated but only for a brief period of time. The chronic use of opioid medications was discouraged, as the risk of addiction was well known.

The benefits of powerful new opioids with fewer side effects were heavily marketed to physicians trained in relieving pain and suffering as part of their job. This made prescribing them seductively easy. Physicians were convinced that using the newer opioids to relieve pain was a better way to take care of their patients. Marketers downplayed the substantial risks of dependency and addiction by lauding the benefits of treating chronic pain. A not-so-subtle generational shift in the threshold for the use of these medications emerged, even though no rigid, evidenced-based medical proof suggested these powerful opioids were superior to traditional care. Something seemed wrong. In fact, recent studies have suggested that there is no benefit to treating chronic pain with opioids, except for pain from cancer.

When I returned home after my hip replacement surgery in October 2014, I had been encouraged to take at least one "Oxy" before PT, but I refused. Following joint replacement, the pain from my left hip was gone. I was gaining strength, mobility, and stamina from the outpatient physical therapy. Unfortunately, I was walking so much, pain from my herniated disc recurred. Paradoxically, as I grew stronger, the increased activity put strain on my spine. The back pain that had resolved with prolonged bedrest resurfaced. Worse yet, I began to trip as my right leg dragged from weakness caused by the herniated disc. This was a new sensation.

Even sitting for more than a short time resulted in back pain. My therapist suggested I use a saddle seat instead of a regular chair or stool. The seat looks like a saddle you would use when riding a horse, set upon a typical stool base without a back or arm rests. This forces the spine to be straight—as it would if you were actually mounted on a horse. This simple innovation and my willingness to adapt helped. I was the subject of merciless teasing, but I didn't care: the pain was less.

The lifestyle-limiting pain prompted me to be evaluated by my neurosurgeon who again offered an invasive option but with the sobering statistic of a 50/50 chance of relief. Stated differently: the odds were 50 percent that I would be better after surgery, or there was a 50 percent chance that the pain would not decrease, along with the real possibility of a potentially worse outcome—more pain, paralysis, and life in a wheelchair. The obverse of the surgeon's motto was apparent: a chance to cut is not always a chance to cure. With either result, the healing would take up to 12 months. It would be an excruciating recovery, so I declined. I continued with lumbar epidural steroid injections, which helped, but with each injection, the degree and duration of pain relief declined.

Someone recommended that I be evaluated by a physiatrist, a specialist in physical and rehabilitative medicine, who does not perform surgery. Though a physician myself, this specialty was largely unknown to me. The same grim 50/50 surgical statistics and 12 months of recovery were quoted, but an alternative suggested next was unexpected: aggressive physical therapy from a group that specializes in spine therapy. The success would be predicated on my ability to withstand what would be painful, dedicated spine physical therapy. My wife and I were skeptical. I had already been through a lot of physical therapy, but the surgical odds were not that great, so I decided to try this before irrevocable surgery was done.

My first day at spine therapy I met with an enthusiastic therapist who performed the most detailed evaluation of my muscle strength and skeletal mobility that anyone had given me. Yes, simply stated, my X-rays and scans revealed that my spine anatomy was somewhere between challenging and a complicated mess. Surgery would improve the appearance of the X-rays, but what I learned from this thorough exam was new: the core muscles of my spine and abdomen had atrophied along with every other muscle when I was intubated and immobile from ARDS. This made complete sense. Up to this point, the goal of therapy had been directed at restoring independence by strengthening the muscles of my legs, hands, and arms, which enabled me to walk, eat, bathe, and dress myself again. Rebuilding my spinal and abdominal core muscles were not the priority, and hence, they remained atrophied. Without the strength of these muscles supporting my spine, the entire weight of my body was focused on the weakest point. No wonder I was in such agony. The plan was to strengthen my core muscles and stretch the contracted tendons and ligaments with the goal being durable alleviation of my pain.

No one overestimated the pain from this spine therapy. It was extreme, but the hope of long-term relief, without the prohibitive risk and uncertain outcome of spine surgery, kept me motivated. The first few weeks were very hard, but I experienced inklings of progress. Pain from muscle spasms in the large back and leg muscles was intense and unrelenting. I felt and walked as if I were 30 years older than I was. My back and thigh muscles were not soft and supple as they were supposed to be but rather felt like rigid steel cables. Just touching them caused pain. Deep tissue massage was recommended. The massage therapist was a registered nurse, and she was honest in stating that the treatment was going to be extremely painful but necessary if the spasms were to resolve. It would be essential for me to have trust and confidence in her. I did, and the deep tissue massage helped.

Next came treatments with stainless steel implements as part of the "Graston" Technique. This procedure is reserved for patients who have fascial scar tissue. It works to decrease muscle inflammation, increase mobility, and relieve pain. Enduring the discomfort needed to release the fascial scar tissue and muscle spasm was not easy, but I had already learned to mentally channel Ben Franklin: "no pain, no gain." My eyes teared up from these treatments, which definitely hurt, but as the constant pain from the muscle spasm faded, I endured.

Finding ways to remain motivated was challenging. Physical therapy was tedious and slow. Visiting the Galapagos Islands was one of my wife's dream trips. She loves birds, animals, and travel. All my life I had been goal oriented. When my efforts slacked, the solution would be to challenge myself with something difficult then be rewarded for attaining what I had set out to achieve. In 2016, I added the audacious goal of hiking at least a part of the Inca Trail, climbing Machu Picchu, and visiting all of the Galapagos Islands. This was the biggest stretch goal ever. Skeptical, my wife made us buy trip insurance before she agreed to the plan. I clipped out a picture of the goal and focused harder than ever.

My therapist showed me how to use walking sticks to help with balance and to ease my body weight off of the spine. I practiced by climbing different trails up to the top of the Blue Hills in Canton, Massachusetts. Following months of aggressive spine therapy, the pain I had lived with for so long had largely improved as did my strength, flexibility, and balance. October 2017, my wife and I arrived in Peru. Not only did I climb Machu Picchu with the help of hiking sticks; I climbed it twice. We walked and swam all over the Galapagos Islands. I returned to work reinvigorated and proud that I had achieved my reach goal.

When I went back to show my physical therapists the picture of me atop the ancient ruins, I asked, "Why do so few people undertake the rigorous spine physical therapy?"

Their response was, in a way surprising, but not really: "When people suffer constant pain and have limited mobility, spine surgery is an easier option, with the easiest option being taking chronic opioids. Committing to and completing rigorous spine physical therapy is the most difficult of these choices. It requires trust, faith, and a deep personal commitment for many months while at the same time, the ability to endure discomfort. The long-term benefits of this choice are superior and also more likely to relieve pain and improve functioning if you continue the life-long home therapy exercises."

Again, the words of Nietzsche reverberated in my head: "He who has a 'why' to live for can bear almost any 'how,' as did his other words: "To live is to suffer, to survive is to find some meaning in the suffering."

One day when waiting for a haircut from my local barber, I thumbed through a 2020 *GQ* magazine and read an article by Zach Barron: "Icon of the Year George Clooney When We Need Him Most." Mr. Clooney related that he had lived with pain for fifteen years. Following near-death from a motorcycle accident, he had taken pain killers. At some point, he was evaluated by a pain specialist who told him, "Pain is the body's way of registering a departure from what it regards as normal. If you train yourself to think of pain as normal, then the pain will cease to exist. The idea is you try to reset your pain threshold. Much of the time what happens with pain is you are constantly mourning for how you used to feel." He stopped using pain killers and reset how he allowed his mind to view pain.

This random read in the most unexpected place was eye opening. I spoke with my physiatrist, who confirmed this concept and recommended that I read more on it. And so I committed to a serious practice of mindfulness meditation to reset my brain's pain threshold. This quest to master mindfulness meditation had begun years earlier with the recommendation by the Brigham Women's Hospital Anesthesia and Orthopedic Service to listen to the Peggy Huddleston tape prior to the total hip replacement. It evolved into a helpful, deep, and long journey.

Chapter 9

Meditation

> *"Over the course of my own meditation practice and of doing the work I do in the world, I have come to see the cultivation of mindfulness as a radical act—a radical act of sanity, of self-compassion, and ultimately, of love."*
> Jon Kabat-Zinn

When I started writing this book, I hadn't planned on including a chapter on meditation. After months of editing and introspection, however, I realized that meditation seemed inseparable from the story. This insight dawned on me late into the process. My hesitancy was that I am not an expert on meditation, and my education continues. Understanding the connection between the mind and chronic pain came with reading and learning ways to practice meditation.

In Buddhist teachings, there are seven basic types of meditation. Just as with Judeo-Christian meditation, there are spiritual or religious aspects to some of these, but one does not have to be a Buddhist to reap the benefits.

1. Mindfulness meditation is the practice of being fully present with our thoughts, aware of where we are and what we are doing, and not being overly reactive to what is going on around or within us.

We observe thoughts and emotions but let them pass without judgement.

2. Transcendental meditation involves a mantra, i.e., a word, sound, or phrase, that is repeated in a specific way for twenty minutes, twice a day, while sitting with eyes closed. This technique allows us to achieve a profound state of relaxation and rest, with the goal of achieving inner peace.

3. Guided meditation is a method in which one forms mental pictures or situations that one finds relaxing.

4. Vipassana meditation was first taught in India 2,500 years ago. The goal is self-transformation through self-observation to establish a deep connection between mind and body. The continuous interconnectedness results in a balanced mind full of love and compassion.

5. Loving-kindness meditation or metta meditation is the practice of directing positive and loving energy to others and oneself.

6. Chakra meditation comes from the ancient Sanskrit word for "wheel." Chakra refers to the seven centers of energy and spiritual power in the body. Chakra meditation is made up of relaxation techniques focused on bringing balance and well-being to the chakras.

7. Yoga meditation has many styles, but all involve performing a series of postures with relaxed, deep breathing—exercises meant to promote flexibility and calm the mind. The poses require balance and concentration. In yoga, you are encouraged to stay in the moment.

Ignatius of Loyola wrote the Spiritual Exercises that "have as their purpose the conquest of self and the regulation of one's life in such a way that no decision is made under the influence of any inordinate attachment." The Exercises teach two primary forms of prayer: meditation and contemplation. With meditation, we use our minds. We think of the basic principles that guide our life. Contemplation is more about feeling than thinking. The Exercises are often practiced in retreats that can last for hours or, in some situations, days. During the Jesuit retreats that I attended at Boston College High School, the importance of examining where you currently are in your life, where you have come from, and where you would like to be next year and in ten years was stressed. We were taught to be intentional rather than reactional with our life decisions.

Meditation has been part of Buddhist and Judeo-Christian teaching for thousands of years. Over the centuries, secular meditation has developed along with spiritual meditation. Dr. David H. Rosmarin, Assistant Professor of Psychology, Harvard Medical School, and the Director of the Spirituality and Mental Health Program at McLean Hospital, noted that prayer may have similar benefits to meditation. It can calm your nervous system, shutting down your flight or fight response (located in the amygdala of the brain). Prayer can make you less reactive to negative emotion and less angry. I found prayer to be calming when I lay intubated in the BWH ICU.

As part of my pre-surgical preparation at BWH, I was introduced to mindfulness meditation. Surprisingly, this was highly effective in diminishing my acute post-op pain and became the catalyst for my quest to learn additional ways to train my mind and control daily chronic pain. I read as much as I could on this subject and twice attended the intense conference, Meditation for Peak Performance and Everyday Living, by Dr. Daniel Brown from Harvard Medical School (in 2016 and 2017). Additionally, I downloaded meditation smart phone apps until I found one that I really liked.

My inquiry led me to the work of Jon Kabat-Zinn, whom I had heard of but regrettably, had not studied his works. He earned his Ph.D. in molecular biology from the Massachusetts Institute of Technology (MIT) and studied under several Zen

Buddhist teachers. He is currently an Emeritus Professor of Medicine at the University of Massachusetts Medical School (UMMS) and is the founder of the Center for Mindfulness in Medicine, Health Care and Society at the UMMS. In his book *Full Catastrophe Living: Using the Wisdom of Your Body and Mind to Face Stress, Pain and Illness,* he describes Mindfulness-Based Stress Reduction (MBSR), as a significant coping method. He merged his training in molecular biology and Zen-Buddhism, then went on to remove Buddhist religious aspects of mindfulness to provide the scientific basis of his MBSR technique. He used "mindful yoga," meditation as an exercise routine devoid of religious connotation. The Center for Mindfulness (CFM) at UMMC offers training in MBSR. Currently, there are more than 700 medical centers and clinics worldwide that utilize it.

Sitting in a cross-legged yoga position to meditate was physically impossible for me, even after hip replacement surgery. I sat in a chair with my feet firmly on the floor and my spine upright though not resting on the back of the chair. My hands were either flat on my thighs or with fingertips gently touching. Progress was very slow, and my mind often wandered. It took a long time to see results, but they came with persistent practice. I meditated for a minimum of 30 minutes every day over the span of six years until I could ignore my pain and that which was going on around me.

For more intrusive thoughts, mindfulness meditation helped me master the skill of "noting." This allows you to put random thoughts off to the side and "note them," thereby preventing the thoughts from disturbing your meditation. This skill fosters the ability to be totally present and not sidetracked by things happening outside yourself or popping into your head. This practice not only helped control my chronic musculoskeletal pain, but it also helped me become a better person and physician. None of my family or friends meditated and were a bit skeptical that it would be of any benefit. They were surprised that I saw results but slowly came around, and some have adopted their own daily meditation practice after seeing the benefits that accrued to me. To this day, I meditate daily.

While an in-patient at Spaulding Hospital, my physical therapists introduced me to yoga. Although I was aware of yoga, I was never attracted to it. This was solely out of ignorance on my part. At first, I really didn't see the value, but after hours of performing a series of yoga postures with controlled breathing (albeit with limited poses due to pain and impaired balance), I understood how these exercises work to calm the mind and promote flexibility. The poses require concentration and good balance. Similar to other skills which take practice over years to get good at and longer to master, it provides benefits along the way.

Similarly, Tai Chi, originally a martial art, is valuable in balance training, something I was in dire need of improving. It, too, requires you to focus your mind and breathing to direct your movements and body-flow sequences. At Spaulding Hospital, it took me an incredibly long time to learn how to breathe properly while exercising (to not hold my breath). I discovered that I was not alone in having to adjust what I'd assumed was a basic respiratory function.

What is the science behind meditation and prayer that it has not only survived but grown in popularity over millennia? First a brief anatomy review. The brain is composed of a number of layers. The cerebral cortex is felt to be where conscious thought, logic, and reason reside. Memories are stored in neural networks found here as well as in other areas of the brain. The prefrontal cortex is the area of the brain that organizes mental and physical activity. All executive functions begin here. This is where we integrate what is happening around us with knowledge and memories stored in other parts of the brain. It delays decisions and action until facts and emotions are processed. The amygdala is the fire alarm of the brain. It recognizes non-verbal information such as facial expression and body position and recalls unpleasant memories that can trigger a strong stress response, thereby highjacking the ability of the prefrontal cortex to process information. This is the "fight or flight" response that saves us from danger but can also lead to less-than-optimal responses due to partially, improperly processed information. The hippocampus balances the amygdala and is associated with resilience. This part of the brain processes facts and helps lead to rational actions rather than reflexive ones. As coping skills are formed, the hippocampus sends this information into our long-term memory and connects it to other memories previously stored.

In chronic pain, the size of the hippocampus shrinks. Regular meditation and aerobic exercise have been shown to increase the size of the hippocampus and conversely decrease the size of the amygdala when measured with MRI imaging. Over-activity of the amygdala has been correlated with greater perception of pain that can overwhelm the ability of the hippocampus to mitigate that perception. In severe chronic pain, hyperactivity of the amygdala can create a high hurdle for exercise and meditation to overcome but not an impossible one.

Evidence-based science supporting the mind-body-pain connection is solid. Regular practice of mindfulness meditation and aerobic exercise make it possible to train the mind so that the focus is no longer on the body's pain. Not surprisingly, this requires a major leap of faith for those hurting, along with a great deal of hard work over many months. I know this from my own personal experience. Through a better understanding of how the amygdala creates a barrier to doing what is needed to lessen non-cancer related pain, we can better devise treatment programs to help those who suffer from chronic pain. Successful, long lasting pain control is correlated with lifelong daily training of the mind and body, just as with any skill.

Overcoming the fear of worsening my back pain with dedicated spine physical therapy was crucial to learning to control what was controlling me. Medically prescribed, supervised, daily exercise coupled with mindfulness meditation lessened my chronic pain. This point is not simply extremely important; it is crucial. *Some exercise will aggravate the pain, so it is critical to follow a program prescribed by a physiatrist or physical therapist.* Whatever you do, you must not make the problem worse. Following improvement in my back pain, I returned to activities such as snow shoveling, bending, and raking. Not surprising, my back pain worsened. After making this mistake several times, I more fully appreciated Albert Einstein's Law of Insanity: expecting a different outcome after doing the same thing over again. It took me a long time to stop digging my hole deeper and climb out. Once I was able to *acknowledge* the fact that my spine was never going to be normal, I was finally able to *accept* this reality over the denial that I was stuck in. It was only then that I was able to successfully *adapt* my activities to avoid causing more pain.

In my numerous years as a physician, I have been saddened by the number of patients who made these same bad choices and entered a cycle of pain and decreased mobility. Subsequent searches for a quick cure with surgery or opioids often leads to more surgery, more opioids, continued pain, and disability. There is no easy recovery button for chronic back pain. It is not possible to get a new spine. However, it is possible to make good choices. It is essential to acknowledge and accept this. Learning to adapt your activities to avoid a negative feedback loop of injury, pain, re-injury, and ever-decreasing mobility is necessary. *A life-long commitment to regular exercise and mindfulness is required.* Even missing two weeks of an exercise program can lead to loss of what had been gained through months of hard work. This was another lesson that I learned the hard way. These setbacks are to be expected as life happens. More structured spine therapy got me back to where I was before re-injuring myself. Anger over the setbacks is a useless emotion and gets in the way of the essential work of resuming the mental and physical exercise that previously helped.

An obstacle to success is the fact that many patients suffering from chronic pain are both physically and emotionally debilitated. It is not unusual for chronic pain patients to have already been evaluated by a number of health care specialists, and not finding relief, feel skeptical of the medical profession. Creating trust by being empathetic is needed to establish the bond required to change the negative feedback loop created by chronic pain. My hope in sharing my story is that at least one person will be helped.

Getting stuck in mourning the past life you had without pain and the inability to move beyond the limitations in your current life will prevent you from embracing what you have or seeing a future with meaning, purpose, and happiness. This is, in essence, a form of locked-in thinking, which creates blinders and has been shown to be the root cause of many medical and military errors. Mourning the past impedes growth, change, and prevents happiness. So, what is needed to embrace an altered future?

Chapter 10

Resilience

"It's your reaction to adversity, not adversity itself that determines how your life's story will develop."
Dieter F. Uchtdorf

Prior to the 1980s, resilience was most commonly used to describe a quality of material and is derived from the Latin "resilire," to leap back. During the 1980s, "resilient" became a popular term when referring to a person. In psychology, the word resilience refers to a person's return to the previous level of functioning following resolution of a major stressor. Colloquially, this is referred to as "bouncing back." Also, prior to the 1980s, the word "tough," or "toughness," was used to describe someone who was able to recover from life's traumas. Now, this word has the more negative connotation of being unrefined or having an edge. Words and their meanings change on a regular basis.

Resilience has long been known to be a critical trait in those who survive and recover from whatever fate life has in store for them. For a long time, conventional wisdom suggested that resilience was something that you were born with but didn't know you had. New research has shown that resilience can be learned. George Vaillant, director of the Study of Adult Development at Harvard Medical School, noted that some people become significantly more resilient over the years, while others become less resilient—suggesting that this can be learned or, conversely, that it can atrophy.

In her research on resilience, Diane L. Coutu noted that most resilience theories had three commonalities: 1) acceptance of reality; 2) a deep value-based belief that life is meaningful; and 3) the ability to improvise. You could recover from whatever life circumstances you encountered with one or two of these traits, but it takes all three to be truly resilient. Interestingly, she noted that this observation held true for organizations as well as individuals.

In three decades as a physician, my observation of patients who successfully overcame whatever life challenge they faced was similar to that of Diane Coutu. When counseling patients, I referred to these qualities as the three A's. You had to achieve all three to successfully surmount whatever hardship you faced.

1. Acknowledge: this requires awareness—without this you can't admit the problem. Unless you acknowledge that which you face, you can't move on to acceptance.
2. Accept: acceptance of the problem is harder still but essential if you are to move past anger and disappointment, which are natural reactions to unwanted problems. Resist denial.
3. Adapt: this is the hardest stage of the three. You must be flexible enough to reinvent yourself, to find your life's purpose and meaning in life again.

There are numerous components to resilience. Learning these skills and practicing them is crucial to attaining your goals—just as you would study for an exam or practice a sport or musical instrument to gain fluid competency. Success is rarely achieved by accident, and lasting success is never accidental.

In the previous chapter on meditation, we learned that the part of the brain associated with resilience is the hippocampus. It plays a major role in learning and memory development and is most strongly associated with resilience. Essentially, it functions as a brake on the amygdala's function of promoting reflexive action. Severe stress leads to elevated levels of cortisol (stress hormone), which overstimulates the amygdala and impairs efficient functioning of the hippocampus thus impeding the brain's ability to concentrate and problem solve.

Regular exercise, a healthy diet, adequate sleep, and avoidance of alcohol and tobacco all help improve brain function needed for resilience. Conversely, any deviation from these healthy lifestyles can create the risk of upsetting the proper balance between the prefrontal cortex, amygdala, and the hippocampus that ensures resilience. Learning to manage stress in life is a crucial skill needed to gain maximal ability to "bounce back." When imbalance in these areas does occur, unwelcome mental health problems such as anxiety, depression, insomnia, phobias, and post-traumatic stress disorders (PTSD) can ensue. Fortunately, the aforementioned healthy-lifestyle suggestions go far to restore balance when it has been lost.

Many writers have spent years researching and teaching resilience; one of the most pre-eminent is Robert J. Wicks, Ph.D., a Professor Emeritus at Loyola University Maryland. A clinical psychologist, he specialized in elucidating the interplay of psychology and spirituality. Early in his career, he developed expertise in substance use disorder, working for the State of New York Narcotic Addiction Commission. Later, he joined the military where he served in the United States Marine Corps. Following the Rwandan Civil War, he helped relief workers process their traumatic experiences. He worked in Cambodia to help those who were assisting survivors of the Pol Pot reign of terror to rebuild their country. Dr. Wicks worked with the American military health care community ministering to Iraqi and Afghan War veterans suffering from multiple amputations and trauma.

In two of his books, *Perspective: The Calm Within the Storm* and *Bounce: Living the Resilient Life,* he reviews knowledge and insight gained from life experience on cognitive behavioral therapy and psychology. He discusses how mindfulness, gratitude, and happiness help us become more aware of the good present in our lives and contribute to developing a more positive perspective. This allows us to maintain emotional balance in spite of the stress that is omnipresent in the world. He details self-care and self-renewal techniques he has successfully used to help others manage stress and to live a more meaningful, resilient, and compassionate life.

My father offered a different approach to developing resilience. He was a stern taskmaster when I was growing up, and typical of most adolescents, I resented it. One day I asked my father why he was so hard on me. He replied, "It's my duty as your father to toughen you up. It's how my father raised me. Life on our farm in Ireland was very hard." He went on to relate that when he was 16 years old, his father had a very difficult talk with him: he calmly stated that there were too many mouths to feed and from that moment, he was on his own to support himself. In 1929, during the Great Depression, this was not such an unusual conversation for a father to have with a son anywhere in the world. "Life is not fair," his father went on to say, "and there is no point in wasting time or energy trying to change what can't be changed. There is no benefit in viewing yourself as a victim when the inevitable hardships of life occur. There will always be tough breaks, someone who is richer, smarter, taller, more athletic, better looking, etcetera. You must play the cards that you are dealt with in life to the best of your ability." My father learned to be resilient, and in turn he taught me, thus filling my life skills toolbox with lessons I needed to survive. He exemplified those words of Confucius: "The greatest glory in living lies not in never falling, but in rising every time we fall."

My father allowed himself to be motivated by his father's words. For many, it feels natural to become enraged at circumstances that knock a person down. Yet, when contemplating how he survived in Auschwitz, Victor Frankl wrote in *Man's Search for*

Meaning, "We must never forget that we may also find meaning in life even when confronted with a hopeless situation, when facing a fate that cannot be changed." We can't avoid suffering but we can choose how we deal with it and move on with life. Anger is very powerful but it is a destructive emotion that gets in the way of happiness and resilience.

Looking back, I am grateful for my father's instruction, as it did prepare me for life, and I tried to pass his wisdom on when raising my own sons. In retrospect, I can acknowledge that these life lessons were among the greatest gifts he gave me. In my father's words: Learn to play the cards you are dealt in life carefully and with skill.

Many years later, I found another of my father's lessons accurately reflected, yet again, by Nelson Mandela, "It is what we make out of what we have, not what we are given, that separates one person from another." He is another inspiring, resilient person whom I have quoted often in this book. In 2017, my wife and I had the pleasure of visiting South Africa, and the most unexpected highlight was visiting the Nelson Mandela Museum. I had an elementary understanding of the history of South Africa, Apartheid, and the story of Nelson Mandela, but the power of the museum in conveying the unvarnished truth of what happened was breathtaking.

Our host treated us to a luncheon with Nelson Mandela's jailor, Christo Brand, who gave us a deeply personal account of Apartheid and how his life was forever transformed by the years he spent as Nelson Mandela's jailor, and how ultimately, Nelson Mandela became his friend and mentor. Later, I spent hours reading about Nelson Mandela's life, how he survived for nearly three decades as political prisoner number 46664. For many of those years, he was housed on an island fortress. Quite remarkably, after his ultimate release, he transformed the prevailing dialogue from one of vengeance to one of forgiveness, peace, and reconciliation. "When a deep injury is done to us, we never heal until we forgive," and "You will achieve more in this world through acts of mercy than you will through acts of retribution," are two of my favorite quotes from him.

He could have exited decades in prison as a hardened, bitter and angry man seeking revenge, but he did not. When asked why, he responded, "Resentment is like drinking poison and then hoping it will kill your enemies." Like Mahatma Gandhi, he left jail convinced in his belief that non-violent resistance was the best path to lasting change. (So, too, did Dr. Albert Schweitzer echo his sentiment: "Just as white light consists of colored rays, so reverence for life contains all the components of ethics: love, kindness, sympathy, empathy, peacefulness, and the power to forgive.") In my mind, the resilience of Nelson Mandela, his powerful message of kindness, humility, and forgiveness, cements him as one of history's greatest leaders.

After I returned to work, I had the opportunity to attend a dinner at Harvard Business School as part of a Brigham and Women's Hospital-sponsored yearlong leadership program that I was enrolled in. The speaker, Dr. Tom Lee, made mention of several books with powerful messages. One was: *Grit: The Power of Passion and Perseverance* by Dr. Angela Duckworth. I made a mental note to read it after I finished the pile of books I was working my way through. The recommendation was spot on. This book really spoke to me; I couldn't put it down. It helped me to better understand what I have observed throughout my own life and recovery but could never find the words to describe.

Even though I lived through what I previously had thought would have been insurmountable and returned to a full life, I could not explain how I did it when so many others couldn't or were only partially able to. In Dr. Duckworth's book, I found that what she wrote about success in business and sports could also apply to anyone recovering from a life-altering illness: "The successful had a ferocious determination that played out in two ways. First, these (individuals) were unusually resilient and hardworking. Second, they knew in a very, very deep way what it was they wanted. They not only had determination, they had direction. It was this combination of passion and perseverance that made (them) special. In a word, they had grit." In addition, she showed that it is possible to become "grittier" with intentional practice. You can train or retrain your brain to be resilient when bouncing back from a major or even minor setback in life.

While studying for her doctoral degree, Angela Duckworth had been challenged by her advisor to develop a theory to explain her observation that being gifted and talented failed to explain achievement. Her research included interviews with highly successful people in various life endeavors. Her remarkable insight was: effort counts twice. She went on to identify an algorithm on how to measure grit as well as to show how a person could learn to develop grit from the inside out then go on to teach this skill to others under your care. The words of my father, "work hard and never quit," again strongly echoed. Interestingly, she posited that you don't have to be "gritty" at everything you try, but you must be focused, persistent, and practice what you want to succeed at. When you quit doing what you have committed to, your effort drops to zero and your skills not only stop improving; they atrophy. Dr. Duckworth's research confirmed Dr. Vailliant's observation that you can become more resilient as you age.

Following a life-altering illness, when a person is in pain and participating in rehabilitation with no guarantee of success in attaining the level of functioning they once had, finding what is possible to achieve can be daunting. It is easy to give up and become a victim of unmet potential. What could have been achieved with more effort and faith in your work ethic becomes what could have been but wasn't. The observation that hard work is more important to success than raw talent is foundational to Dr. Duckworth's research. After my second near-death experience and prolonged hospitalization, I could no longer complete my daily exercises. My back pain returned and limited me even further. I knew what I needed to do in order to restore the strength and endurance that I lost. Once I was strong enough, I resumed my physical therapy with zeal. At each level of mastery, I pushed myself past my comfort zone, stretching my goals beyond what I had previously achieved.

Dr. Duckworth writes, "Grit has two components: passion and perseverance, both scored separately. Most people have a higher perseverance than passion score." My passion score exceeded that of my perseverance score, though not by much. Many of the people that Dr. Duckworth interviewed noted that consistency over time was crucial to accomplishing their life goals. Increasing my exercise time and the level of intensity were my lower-level building blocks. In her research she identified practice compared with *deliberate* practice and why this is so important for success. Brute-force practice does not lead to the desired improvement. The requirements for deliberate, mindful practice in achieving excellence were:

- A clearly defined stretch goal
- Full concentration and effort
- Immediate and informative feedback
- Repetition with reflection and refinement

When I look back, I realize that my physical and occupational therapists at Spaulding Rehabilitation gave me the needed components to master deliberate practice in my quest to rebuild my body. It helps if you have previously developed a structured daily activity of something either in school, athletics, music, or sports, but it is not essential. I have cared for many patients who smoked, were overweight, and who did no regular exercise yet survived life-threatening heart attacks followed by coronary artery revascularization. Those patients who completed structured cardiac rehabilitation, followed by a personal commitment to deliberate regular exercise, lived longer and achieved a much higher level of functioning than those who did not.

Inspiration from people who have risen above mountainous obstacles, as well as personal experience, has taught me that effort and perseverance are essential to recovering from a life-altering trauma. It was Dr. Duckworth that helped me understand that the life lessons of hard work and resiliency learned decades earlier from my father and eight years of Jesuit education explained how I was able to not only survive but to thrive.

Life's Purpose and Meaning

> *"The two most important days in your life are*
> *the day you are born and the day you find out why."*
> Mark Twain

In the spring of 2014, following my discharge from Spaulding Hospital, the hard reality of the situation I faced was inescapable. The good news was that I had survived ARDS and myriad complications. Rediscovering my life's purpose and its meaning were important but seemed unimaginably difficult when even the smallest physical activity was exhausting and painful. Confused, I wondered if *any* part of the life I had known before this illness would be retrievable. How long my recovery would take or the degree to which my health and functioning would be restored was unknown.

My goal of making it home had been achieved. I was beyond grateful to be alive, but my body had to be rebuilt. As mentioned earlier, days began with three hours of self-directed physical therapy followed by rest, lunch, study, then another two hours of exercise. The workouts were divided between upper body, lower body, and core strengthening. I pushed myself hard, just as though my life depended on it, which in fact it did. Progress was glacially slow, almost imperceptible when measured in days. The phrase "Herculean effort," took on a more nuanced meaning.

At times I felt as though I was in a mental fog. Problem solving that had been rapid, even split second, seemed to be in slow motion. The importance of staying mentally sharp was essential. I read medical books, journals, and completed as many online courses as I could find. My evenings were spent devouring books, bought or received as gifts, on survival and recovery. The search for insight on how to recover was always top of mind. Copious note-taking was a deeply ingrained habit that reflexively took over (and helped me greatly when writing this memoir). The lessons these books held inspired as well as challenged me. The stories portrayed the amazing ability of humans to overcome extreme, even unimaginable, life traumas. The question I faced was, could I? They gave me hope.

It gradually became self-evident that I was not going to be able to return to caring for my patients when they were at their sickest, hospitalized, or requiring intensive care. Although caring for the sickest of the sick was physically demanding, it brought me joy and immense satisfaction. This was something that I had been doing for over three decades, creating an intense bond with my patients and their families. I realized that it gave me more meaning and purpose than I had appreciated. When some of my patients decided to switch their care to physicians who could follow them in the hospital as well as the office, I understood. But honestly, it wounded me. Being an office-based-only physician was my new reality, and I was unsure if this would be enough. I struggled to decide if I should pivot to administration, teaching, or something else entirely. *But what could offer fulfillment for the rest of my life?*

Over the centuries, scholarly works by theologians, philosophers, psychiatrists, and psychologists have exhaustingly explored "life's purpose" and its corollaries, "life's meaning" and "happiness." The publication of hundreds of articles and books echoing those queries continues, underscoring the enormous interest in understanding these concepts. Having your life's purpose forcibly taken from you by illness (or for that matter, any reason) can potentially remove your reason for being. The inability to return to what makes your life meaningful can leave you unmoored, spiraling into a personal existential crisis. Before this happens, it is imperative to contemplate a replacement for your prior, purposeful passion. On average, people who feel connected to a strong life purpose have an associated increase in longevity.

The memory of my Greek philosophy courses at Boston College High School and Boston College reminded me of a small but powerful book, *The Enchiridion*. Essentially, it is a manual of the highlights of the teachings of Stoic philosopher, Epictetus, compiled by one of his students. (The main body of his work is in *The Discourses of Epictetus*.) Aristocrats from the nearby regions sent their children, the future leaders, to learn from the greatest philosopher of the age (70 A.D). One of my favorite lessons is when he lectured that, "Disease is an impediment to the body, but not the will, unless the will itself chooses. Lameness is an impediment to the leg, but not to the will. And add this reflection on the occasion of everything that happens; for you will find it an impediment to something else, but not to yourself."

Epictetus was born into slavery. It is believed that his leg was injured at a young age and never properly healed, leaving him disabled. Thus, he showed us through his own life experience that you have the ability to choose how you react to events. Ultimately, you are in control of how you respond to all of your life circumstances. This concept was more deeply explored by Viktor Frankl who concluded that the "will to meaning" is the basic motivation for humanity. This concept became the cornerstone of his school of psychology that he termed logotherapy. The word is derived from the Greek word *logos*, which translates to "meaning," and "therapy," which is treatment of a condition.

As mentioned earlier, both Frankl and his wife were sent to Nazi concentration camps. His life's work, the textbook on logotherapy, was confiscated upon arrival at Auschwitz. It was love for his wife (who had perished, unbeknownst to him) and the goal of rewriting this book that sustained him during the three years spent as a concentration camp inmate. It became his life's "purpose." His observation of those with the best chance of surviving life in the concentration camps were those who found something meaningful to live for. If prisoners lost hope, many died. "Any attempt to restore a man's inner strength in the camp had first to succeed in showing him some future goal. Whenever there was an opportunity for it, one had to give them a 'why—an aim' in order to strengthen them to bear the terrible 'how' of their existence."

Despite acknowledging that I had to replace the meaning and purpose that I had found in caring for seriously ill patients, I struggled with accepting this. The future was difficult to envision. Depression took hold of me. I felt myself drifting into an uncomfortable place. It was during this time that I recalled the writing of Thomas Merton, who wrote movingly of his experience with similar issues. Born in France to an American mother and New Zealander father, he converted to Catholicism in 1938 and went on to become a Trappist monk, prolific writer, theologian, mystic, poet, and social activist. Although he wrote over 50 books, the two that I had read (in the 1960s and 1970s) were *The Seven Story Mountain* and *No Man Is an Island*. I recently re-read them. Still powerful. *The Seven Story Mountain* is his autobiography, detailing his spiritual journey of self-discovery. In 1999, *The National Review* listed it as among the 100 best non-fiction books of the century. He wrote that no matter how terrible a man's despair may become, as long as he continues to be a man, his very humanity continues to tell him that life has "meaning." Although the "meaning" may escape us, our purpose in life is to discover and live by it. His deeply insightful words spoke to me in a profound way and helped me overcome the despondency and inertia that was taking root within me.

Similarly, I felt supported in my quest to heal and rediscover my purpose by the observations of Norman Cousins. His 1979 best-selling book, *Anatomy of an Illness as Perceived by the Patient,* recounted his story of a debilitating illness and the many years it took for him to recover. He described the undeniable power of a person's strong will to live, the unshakable belief that somehow, they would recover, no matter how much suffering was crucial to that recovery and had to be endured. This mindset accurately reflected the visceral reality of what I felt as a patient but was unable to put into words during my illness. I must admit that his perspective is something that I have witnessed as a physician but could never understand: how some patients survive against all odds, undergo incomprehensible suffering, yet others give up and die. Every person has a limit to the pain and loss that they can bear. This is not a judgement but an observation of life.

Cousins discussed the connection between creativity and longevity, using as examples, Pablo Casals and Dr. Albert Schweitzer. He met Pablo Casals shortly before his ninetieth birthday and described him as appearing frail but strong in spirit, consumed with his own creativity and desire to accomplish a specific "purpose." The will to live, purpose, faith, and good humor enabled him to perform as a cellist and conductor well into his nineties. Casals went on to discuss his belief that the most serious part of the problem with achieving world peace was that individuals felt helpless to do anything meaningful. His answer to this helplessness was that each person has inside of him (or her) a basic decency and goodness that if listened to and acted on, can give the world a great deal of what it needs most. Treating others with decency and goodness is not a complicated challenge, but it takes tremendous personal courage.

What a wise and uplifting message: every single person has the ability to make a difference in this world. You don't have to be highly educated, a gifted athlete, a famous actor, or powerful to make the world a better place. Leading by example, treating others with basic decency, respect, and goodness is all that is needed.

Cousins went on to describe his meeting with Dr. Albert Schweitzer, also in his nineties, at the hospital Dr. Schweitzer had opened in 1913 in Lambarene, French Equatorial Africa (later Gabon). He had won the Nobel Prize in 1952 for his work there and ran it until his death in 1965. Dr. Schweitzer loved music as did Pablo Casals, especially Bach, and both men shared a sense of humor. Cousins could feel Dr. Schweitzer's essence as having "purpose" and creativity.

The more I read, the better I appreciated that meaning and purpose can be achieved in all stations of life. In 1961, President John F. Kennedy visited NASA for the first time. He was getting the grand tour of the space center when he stopped to speak to a janitor he had spotted mopping the floor. He asked him what he did at NASA, and the man replied, "I'm helping put a man on the moon!" This man clearly understood his "purpose" and that even as a janitor at NASA, what he was doing had "meaning." His answer underscored how he valued his contribution.

With regard to life's purpose and how randomly it can be discovered, Epictetus lectured,

"Remember that thou art an actor in a play of such a kind as the teacher (author) may choose; if short, of a short one; if long, of a long one: if he wishes you to act the part of a poor man, see that you act the part naturally; if the part of a lame man, of a magistrate, of a private person (do the same). For this is your duty, to act well the part that is given to you; but to select the part, belongs to another." In this lesson, we are taught that sometimes life's purpose may not be actively chosen, but rather something that is thrust upon an individual, just as when an average person becomes a hero under unexpected and unplanned circumstances or when someone who has suffered a catastrophic life event finds a way to move forward.

Of the many powerful stories that I read while recovering, one deeply resonated. *The Ice Bucket Challenge* told the story of Pete Frates and his fight against ALS. Pete was a graduate of Boston College, as was I, but unlike me, Pete was a gifted athlete and captain of the BC baseball team. Following graduation, he took an entry-level job and, unsurprisingly, soon wondered what direction his life would take. Pete kept up his passion for baseball, and early on asked his former BC baseball coach, Mike Gambino, if he had any chance at pro ball. After a series of tests, Mike Gambino honestly told him that he didn't have the skills needed to make it to the big league. Unfazed, Pete still had the desire to play baseball competitively. So, he followed his passion and spent a year in Germany playing semi-professionally for the Hamburg Steelers. When he returned home, he took another job but still did not feel the fulfillment he longed for.

Pete Frates' health mysteriously declined, and at age 27, he was diagnosed with ALS (amyotrophic lateral sclerosis), a disease without treatment or cure at that time. ALS is a progressive, rare, and fatal neurodegenerative disease that attacks the nerve cells and their pathways to the brain and spinal cord. Life expectancy is two to five years. For a long time, ALS was synonymous with Lou Gehrig, a famous New York Yankees baseball player who died from it before he reached the age of 38. When given this terminal diagnosis, Pete did not turn inward and wither, which would have been completely understandable, even expected. Rather, he was able to successfully acknowledge, accept, and adapt to the situation he found himself in. There was no time for pity or anger.

At the time of Pete's diagnosis, little research was being done on ALS. His friends and family became despondent over the diagnosis and lack of treatment options. However, Pete Frates became energized when he realized that he had found his life's "purpose." With the force of his will, he rallied his loved ones with the same passion that he rallied teammates when they were behind in a baseball game. He encouraged them to adopt the then largely unknown "Ice Bucket Challenge" as a fundraiser to advance ALS research and raise global awareness of this fatal illness. The young, tech-savvy group merged the power of the Internet with video, and together they electrified the world. Pete had jump-started research into this orphan disease with this massive fundraising effort even while his health steadily declined. When he became immobile and confined to a wheelchair, he continued to be the natural leader that he was, motivating others suffering from ALS and millions of people around the world who loved them. Between July and August of 2014, his "Ice Bucket Challenge" went viral and raised $160 million. By 2017, it had raised $220 million.

Toward the end of his life, things got rough for Pete and his family. He went on to develop the "locked in" phase of ALS where he could no longer communicate. Pete's family learned to communicate by reading his eyes and expressions, just as my wife Colleen and Valentine, in *The Count of Monte Cristo*, did. Pete Frates died on December 9, 2019. In the course of his brief time on earth, he lived and breathed the Jesuit imperative of being a "man or woman for others." Pete's fundraising was instrumental in moving the needle on ALS research and treatment. He made a difference in the world. Pete Frates was and remains my hero. As Albert Einstein said in a *New York Times* interview in 1932, "Only a life lived for others, is the life worthwhile."

Two other stories of people whose physical abilities had been greatly compromised due to unexpected life events inspired me to be open to seeking new avenues in my quest to find meaning and purpose in my life. The actor Christopher Reeve, who starred in the *Superman* series, was paralyzed from the neck down in a tragic horse-riding competition. At some point, he moved past that which could not be changed and devoted his life and energy to his family and to raising money for research on the treatment of spinal cord injury. Similarly, Travis Roy, a hockey player for Boston University, suffered a devastating injury 11 seconds into his first college game that left him paralyzed from the neck down. Similarly, he was also able to dedicate his life and energy to raising money for spinal cord research. Sadly, he recently passed away on October 29, 2020, but the legacy of the Travis Roy Foundation continues.

Carl Jung observed, "The least of things with a meaning is worth more in life than the greatest of things without it." Interestingly, "purpose" and "meaning" do not equal happiness or fulfillment. In the August 1, 2013 issue of the *Atlantic*, Emily Esfahanin Smith succinctly stated: "Meaning is healthier than happiness." Yet, having meaning and purpose coupled with happiness creates balance in life.

Discovering one's purpose or meaning does not guarantee happiness. Being happy is about feeling good. "Meaning" is derived from contributing to others or to society in a bigger way. Aristotle taught that happiness without meaning or purpose is hedonistic. Conversely, it is also possible to have meaning and purpose without happiness. So, my Olympian challenges were: could I identify a path to once again experience those qualities to my life, and would I ever feel truly happy again?

Chapter 12

Happiness

"Success is not the key to happiness.
Happiness is the key to success."
Albert Schweitzer

Viktor Frankl stated that finding purpose and meaning in your life does not guarantee that you will find happiness. Wow! I found that to be a very unsettling thought. Purpose and meaning give you a reason to get out of bed in the morning, but it does not necessarily lead to happiness. So what does lead to happiness?

When I was strong enough to return to work, the meaning and purpose I hoped would return was rekindled; however, much had changed for me. The happiness that I had known before my illness seemed ephemeral. Constant pain, fatigue, and muscle weakness were ever-present reminders of the need to pace myself and limited what I could do. I had to force myself to fight back against the frustration these limitations caused, and honestly, it was exhausting.

Return to work helped bring back the meaning and purpose that being a physician gave me, but the feeling of happiness that I had known prior to my illness seemed more elusive and harder to find. I was beyond grateful to be alive and home with my wife, as well as being with my family and friends. The realization that the inalterable limitations wrought by my catastrophic illness made it impossible for me to return to the rigorous hospital work that had been an inseparable part of my life as a physician began to sink in. There was no missing limb, but it felt as though some part of me was no longer there. The sadness at times overwhelmed me, but it was due to an inescapable fact that could not be altered. It left a void, and I found myself all too frequently mourning this loss. There had to be a way to rekindle happiness, and my goal was to find it.

The more I researched this topic, the more I realized that the problem was not confined to me alone. In an effort to broaden my understanding of happiness, I read as much as I could on the topic and was dismayed to see the results of a 2017 Harris poll survey. It reported that only 33 percent of Americans, one of the wealthiest and most advanced countries in the world, said that they were happy. This prompted curiosity about the disconnect between what makes a person happy and what makes a person unhappy? The Merriam-Webster definition of happiness is "a state of well-being and contentment." Why is this state so hard to achieve?

This quest to understand happiness forced me to look deep within myself. It forced me to become more introspective and face head on that which was impeding my own. The more I delved into this happiness conundrum, the more I began to realize that one could never be happy if they were living in the past, nor could one be happy in the present if they were constantly comparing themselves to others. If you spend too much time imagining the future, you lose today. For me the realization was that I felt meaning and purpose when helping others but yet I felt unhappy because I could not go back to doing all that I previously did, which could not be changed.

This became a personal quest to better understand myself and to articulate that which was unsaid but critically important to my own happiness. The message that I had given my patients for years I gave to myself: Acknowledge the facts as they are, Accept that I have entered a new and unexpected phase of my life, and Adapt to the reality. This helped me greatly in this journey. It was the realization that happiness is being fully present in the moment. It requires the daily acknowledgement of being grateful for what you have and for those you love. I found that there are many ways to build happiness.

Scholars going back nearly three millennia have struggled with the question of how to find happiness. Siddhartha Gautama of Shakya (later known as Buddha), was born in Lumbini near present-day Nepal and northern India about 563 BC though the exact date is disputed. His was a life of wealth and privilege, but he was troubled by what he saw in the world. He left his secure and unburdened life in order to discover how such poverty and cruelty could coexist with the life of privilege he had known.

Following extensive travel and meditation, Siddhartha taught what has become known as the Four Noble Truths and the Eightfold Path to Happiness. He shares wisdom on how to achieve happiness and peace of mind, including teachings on the highest state attainable known as "total consciousness."

Over 2,300 years ago, Aristotle wrote two books describing his theory of happiness. In The Nicomachean Ethics and in The Eudemian Ethics, he asks: What is the ultimate purpose of human existence? His answer is that happiness is the central purpose of human life, and he speaks of the pursuit of happiness in two distinct ways. The first, called "eudaimonic," he regards as preferable, the ultimate value of a life well lived to its fullest potential. This happiness depends on developing moral character and living a virtuous life. The Greek word for happiness is "eudaimonia." The second he calls "hedonic," an in-the-moment, self-centered, pleasure-seeking life. Hedonic life is one without ethics or virtue.

In the book The Art of Happiness by psychologist Howard Cutler and the Dalai Lama, they review the modern scientific basis of happiness and cross reference it to the close to 3,000 years of Buddhist teaching on happiness. Cutler, too, describes happiness and pleasure as being two different things. In making difficult life choices, it helps to reframe one's options as to whether your decision will bring you happiness or pleasure. Purposely choosing happiness is an attitude of embracing life. Pleasure is fleeting.

It is easily observed in life that happiness helps to create a positive feedback loop whereas sadness tends to create a negative feedback loop. For example, when you are surrounded by happy people, the happiness is infectious. Conversely, when you are with sad people, the tendency is to bring the collective mood down. It is natural to be drawn to happy people. They exude a positive attitude even when what is going on around them or in their personal life is not going well. Optimistic people have been shown to be happier and healthier than pessimists.

I witnessed the power of this mindset firsthand as a patient on the spinal cord floor at Spaulding Hospital. The entire staff exuded a positive yet realistic attitude every day on every shift, which permeated the floor. Just as laughter is contagious, so is happiness, and I would add so, too, is a positive attitude. Happiness is a crucial component to resilience. It is possible to reconnect to feeling happy even after unspeakable loss, but you first must open your heart, your mind, and embrace the present and let go of the past, as the past cannot be changed.

Research by Sonia Lyubomirsky has identified three sources associated with happiness. Ten percent of happiness is associated with life circumstances (including marriage, seen to increase happiness and lifespan). Approximately 40 percent of happiness comes from intentional activities. Up to 50 percent of happiness appears to be inherited and thus can't be changed. However, happiness can be influenced. So, while we may be born with genetic traits which can't be altered, most skills and attitudes can be improved by intentionally and regularly practicing activities which bring about feelings of happiness. Happiness comes from being content with what you have and not dwelling on what you lost or never had. Affirming this daily is crucial to being happy.

The demonstration of "neural plasticity" has scientifically proven that the brain can build neural pathways by using regular happiness exercises. Yes, there are happiness exercises, and they work! Practicing new ways of thinking builds neural pathways and remodels the way our brains work. This learning is age independent and underscores the belief that it is never too late to learn. Just as mastering a new language develops identifiable areas of the brain as seen on MRI scans, so it is with training the brain for happiness. This is a critically important scientific finding with substantial real-life implications.

Glenn Schiraldi in *The Resilience Workbook* describes how the use of keeping gratitude journals, writing thank you notes, and verbally sharing happy experiences are simple yet purposeful exercises that build gratitude. Just as healthy eating, regular exercise, and adequate sleep are vital habits for individual wellness, so is the regular practice of gratitude for personal happiness. At the end of a busy day when you and everyone else are exhausted, the words, "thank you for all you did today," when sincerely said to those you toiled with that day, are powerful. Offering heartfelt gratitude while looking directly into the eyes of the person you are addressing is an uplifting experience, both for the person receiving the words and for the person saying them. Happiness exercises when practiced daily and intentionally, just as with a sport or a musical instrument, leads to mastery.

Hence, happiness is determined more by one's state of mind or attitude than by external events. Researchers have shown that the elation of lottery winners and the sorrow of those who have suffered tragic events wanes over time. After a period of adjustment, they often return to their baseline level of day-to-day happiness. Moment to moment happiness is largely determined by one's outlook. Happiness has little to do with our absolute condition but is rather a function of how satisfied we are with what we have. Our feeling of contentment is strongly influenced by our tendency to compare. Constant comparison to those we perceive as having more breeds envy and unhappiness and can become a toxic habit. Interestingly the converse is true. If we compare ourselves to those who have less, this increases our feeling of satisfaction. There is scientific evidence that shifting one's perspective or attitude by contemplating how things could be worse leads to a happier life.

The Dalai Lama stresses that the greater the level of calmness in our minds, the greater our peace of mind, which is rooted in affection and compassion. Meditation is a useful tool to master in order to reach this calmness. Inner contentment comes from appreciating what we have. Modern cognitive behavioral therapy comes closest to the Dalai Lama's suggested training of the mind for happiness. My personal experience has led me to believe that learning the skill of cognitive behavioral therapy is a crucial tool for finding happiness after trauma. Mental outlook is more effective in achieving happiness than accumulating possessions or status in life, which is often fleeting. It's reflected in the 1964 hit song "Can't Buy Me Love," written by Sir Paul McCartney: true and lasting happiness depends on the mind and heart and can't be purchased.

My experience while on a medical missionary trip to Saint Rock, Haiti, confirmed the truth of this observation. Although exhausted after a week of nonstop work caring for impoverished, desperately ill patients, I left Haiti with a sense of joy and accomplishment that I had rarely experienced. In order to be happy, your mental outlook is critical. If you harbor hate, jealousy, or anger, it corrodes all that is good in your life.

The actor, Michael J. Fox, who starred in the movie *Back to the Future*, commented that when he was at a very low point in his life, suffering from the ravages of advanced Parkinson's Disease, he wondered if he had lost his natural optimism. He began to binge-watch old comedy shows and movies from the 1970s. They helped him regain his lost optimism. Similarly, Norman Cousins in *Anatomy of an Illness* described the therapeutic effect of watching old comedies and movies from the 1930s and 1940s. In the biography of Sir William Osler by William Harvey, he advised his physicians that laughter is indeed good medicine. He realized that optimism is rooted in being grateful for what you have and not in what you no longer had or possibly never had. What came next was acceptance of your life as it is and the happiness that arises from feeling satisfied. This is a crucial life lesson that can't be stressed enough.

The Dalai Lama and Howard Cutler cite research by Dr. Linda Wilson, who concluded that altruism may be part of our survival instinct. Once we conclude that the basic nature of humanity is to find happiness, we can accept that altruism, the selfless giving to others, is also associated with happiness and resilience. Furthermore, the practice of selfless giving has been shown to improve happiness more than any other activity. Additional observational proof comes from Dr. Vaillincourt's thirty-plus year longitudinal study of Harvard College graduates that found that altruism was a critical component of good mental health.

One day, my reading led me to an article on a happiness course offered at Yale. In 2018, Yale Psychology Professor Laurie Santos offered a new course, PSYC 157: Psychology and the Good Life. She was motivated to initiate this class out of concern for the level of stress and other mental health issues she witnessed as Head of Silliman Residential College at Yale. The course was designed to help students better cope. It became an instant must-attend course and set the record as the most popular class ever offered at Yale when over 1,200 students, nearly one quarter of the entire undergraduate student population, registered for its inaugural semester. The course (with required reading and commitment to the semester-duration for maximum benefit) for those not attending Yale is currently offered online @coursera.com to anyone who registers. The overwhelming demand suggests that there is a profound need for guidance on finding happiness and work-life balance not only among college students but adults worldwide.

Modern psychology has provided scientific evidence confirming the observations of philosophers and theologians made as far back as thousands of years regarding activities and things that make us happier and those that do not. Here are six lessons from a 2018 interview for *Today* that Professor Santos recommended be used:

1. Spend time and energy the right way. What makes us happy is real life, face-to-face social interactions, not time spent on social media or in a powerful or prestigious job chasing more money. Conversely, research suggests that being on social media is more often associated with anxiety and depression. She underscored the importance of the concept of time affluence—protecting free time from whatever gets in the way of enjoying leisure.

2. Take time to express gratitude. Finding just 10 minutes a day to think about five things you are grateful for can improve your appreciation for what matters and will improve your sense of well-being. As part of this exercise, you must take the time to reflect on what your life would be like without these five things.

3. Do something nice for someone else. Those who engage in random acts of kindness have been shown to boost their emotional well-being.

4. Find time to be mindful, using loving-kindness meditation.

5. Get adequate exercise and sleep.

6. Practice these happiness exercises daily. Improving your emotional well-being is possible, but it takes consistent, intentional work.

One of the most memorable quotes I came across in my reading was from Albert Schweitzer: "Success is not the key to happiness. Happiness is the key to success. If you love what you are doing, you will be successful. The purpose of human life is to serve and to show compassion and the will to help others. I don't know what your destiny will be, but one thing I know: the only ones among you who will be really happy are those who have sought and found a way to serve."

The acceptance of the belief that the purpose of life is to seek happiness is foundational and creates a common bond with all of humanity. The ability to shift perspective, to place oneself in another's shoes, helps create empathy and allows us to better understand divergent views. Compassion is based on the belief that all human beings wish to avoid suffering and be happy. With this insight, we learn to discard the things that lead to suffering and accumulate the things that lead to happiness. I found this to be yet another affirmation that we are all "our brother's keeper."

In a speech given by Nelson Mandela, he stated: "What counts in life is not the mere fact that we have lived. It is what difference we have made in the lives of others that will determine the significance of the life we lead." All humans have a limited time alive, and it is important to make the best use of this time. It is in serving others that we in turn find happiness.

In summary, my quest to find the happiness that I thought I had lost was still present. It never left me, though it took time, honest introspection, and discipline to uncover where it lay buried under the multiple life traumas of the prior years. Happiness was something that I had never given much conscious thought to in the past. It had always seemed natural, and not feeling happy left me confused even though my life had meaning and purpose.

My reading and the lessons I learned from Aristotle, Howard Cutler, the Dali Lama, Glenn Schiraldi, Laurie Santos, and others helped me to understand and articulate that finding happiness was on me. Learning the skill of cognitive behavioral therapy was crucial in my journey. The daily exercise of reframing negative thoughts, of focusing on the present versus the immutable past, and being fully present were some of the strategies I used. Becoming free from the tendency to dwell on the past, on that which was forever gone, took more inner strength than I imagined it would to overcome, but I was able to succeed.

Practicing these happiness exercises daily did work, but like all exercise it required conscious effort and dedicated time. The realization that I had agency—through these happiness exercises—was a breakthrough. That I could choose to use my limited time and energy purposely was a powerful insight.

Keeping a daily journal of five things that I was grateful for and then imagining how my life would be without them became a very impactful tool for me. No matter how chaotic the day was, every day that I worked, I went out of my way to say thank you to the people I worked with. Daily regimented exercise helped relieve my chronic pain, increase my energy level and endurance. Mindfulness meditation became part of my pre-bedtime wind down and led to restful sleep. The nightmares that had been a problem starting when I was near death and later when I was an inpatient at Spaulding Rehabilitation Hospital stopped.

The essence of thousands of years of philosophical and psychological writing is that happiness can be attained through purposeful action but that it takes a long time and requires constant practice. No one can give this to you, and you can't buy it. Happiness comes from within.

Critical to this is the need to be honest with yourself when identifying those factors in life that lead to happiness and those that cause you suffering. The process of introspection does not happen overnight. If you are starting from a position of deep unhappiness, this process can take years and may require professional help. However, with each milestone of awareness, the improvement in your state of happiness is worth celebrating. I can state this because personal experience has shown me that it is possible to find happiness despite illness, personal loss, and near death.

Chapter 13

PTSD

"What we change inwardly will change outer reality."
Plutarch

This chapter on post-traumatic stress disorder (PTSD) is one of the last in my book, but in many ways it's one of the most important. This health issue was the final hurdle to overcome on my road to recovery. I am rather chagrined to admit that even the realization that I suffered from PTSD was so difficult to acknowledge and harder still to write about. Overcoming the shame I felt when I first faced this undeniable truth was daunting. Why was that, and how did I move beyond it?

Denial comes to mind, but it is more than that. I was brought up in an era when memories of trauma or harsh life experiences were things you didn't talk about. You locked them inside a sturdy box then threw it into the deepest canyons of your brain, flinging the key as far away as you could in the opposite direction, hoping they would never be found. This worked until the time they unexpectedly and explosively reunited.

In the 1960s, as a member of the "baby boomer generation," any sign of emotional weakness was better suppressed. The consequences were being ostracized and bullied socially and physically by your peers. Loneliness, beatings, and isolation were just too steep a penalty for sharing the experience. Bottling the feelings up was the path of survival. School counselors were rare to non-existent during this era and if present, unaware of PTSD. To be told you needed to see a psychiatrist was like being branded with arguably something worse than the proverbial "Scarlett Letter." Being diagnosed with a mental illness or told that you were a "head case" was to be avoided at all costs. As a country and as a world community we have a history of failing miserably at providing adequate mental health care to our children and adults. It is not surprising we are reaping the whirlwind.

Looking back on my life, this was clearly unhealthy learned behavior, but it was more than that. Hollywood movies, at that time, glorified war and contributed to the culture of the "tough, macho man" who can get through anything, with barely a lick of emotion or tears shed. Likewise, it was embodied in our personal role models, returning veterans of World War II. My father and his closest Irish immigrant friends who experienced combat never spoke openly of their war experience. They always found time to go to the local VFW Halls to have a "beer and a ball," otherwise known as a "boiler maker," with other veterans, but I never knew what they talked about. Maybe they reminisced about the war, or maybe it was simply the camaraderie of being with fellow survivors, each hoping to find a safe haven.

I recall, when I was a child, finding an old cigar box deep inside our attic that held ribbons and medals from World War II. Some my father had earned; others had been my mother's brother's. Inside was the gold star that my mother had been given in recognition of the death of my uncle, the last surviving male in her family. The box was again put away and never discussed.

As a physician caring for patients, I noted the same patterns of coping with trauma that I assimilated. PTSD was not well understood and not yet taught when I was in medical school, even in the 1970s. Mental health concerns were awkward and avoided. The most difficult things to discuss with patients, I was usually told that they were "no-go zones" if the patient-physician relationship was to continue. I consciously left these discussions for another day for when the patient was ready to broach them.

Two memories of this situation stand out. The first is that of a patient who walked with his knees locked at a 45-degree angle. He stated that it was a war injury that was cared for at the VA and he didn't want me to ask any more questions on the subject. The VA had done all that could be done to fix the problem. After many years, and only when he was near death, did he share with me that he was a survivor of the Bataan Death March and details of the torture he had endured.

The second story was from the wife of a patient who had spent his entire post-World War II life in a locked psychiatric ward at the VA. I never met her husband, but she showed me his picture in military uniform. Although she faithfully visited him until he passed away, all she was told was that he had lost his mind and was a danger to himself, society, and her. She never understood why the military never told her what exactly happened that caused this change in him. Whenever she asked, the answer was always the same: "It's classified." She never remarried and never learned the cause of his condition.

Identification and treatment for the mental conditions which resulted from trauma took decades to coalesce. The term "shell shock" was first used in 1915 by Charles Myers during World War I to describe soldiers who, after experiencing combat, exhibited signs of anxiety, difficulty sleeping, paranoia, and nightmares. Many of these soldiers were stigmatized and incorrectly treated for schizophrenia. During World War II, the term was replaced by "combat fatigue." The numbers of those affected grew exponentially. Many soldiers viewed this disorder as a sign of weakness, blamed themselves, and hesitated to seek what meager mental health resources were available. Self-medication with alcohol and opioids all too often became the norm.

Unfortunately, progress and acknowledgement of this devastating war-related illness did not occur until after the Vietnam War. It is estimated that a staggering 700,000 Vietnam veterans suffered from various forms of PTSD. Substance abuse, compulsive behavior, increased anger or isolation, and the inability to focus and concentrate were among other behavior patterns identified. Homelessness and unemployment also became a growing problem for veterans who desired isolation or exhibited social behaviors that made living in a community an unsolvable challenge. Shifting from stigmatization of those suffering from PTSD to compassion and treatment has been a slow process.

I'm sure I've made clear that in addition to the actual PTSD symptoms I needed to heal, my ingrained attitude regarding vulnerability would need to change as well. The acronym PTSD, though largely associated with war, is currently understood as a response to trauma and abuse and has recently been identified as a complication of life-threatening illness. In addition to the patients themselves, family members and healthcare workers are also vulnerable to PTSD.

So, what is PTSD? In essence, it is a disorder of the recovery process from trauma. Common symptoms include mood swings, fear, anxiety, sadness, hopelessness, nightmares, flashbacks, trouble sleeping, intrusive thoughts and perseveration on death and dying. It is common to experience many of these symptoms after a traumatic event, but for most they should resolve as recovery happens. Thus, PTSD is a continuum of symptoms with some patients requiring no formal treatment and others who not only need therapy but medication as well as social support. If the symptoms persist past one month, it suggests that recovery is not occurring as it should. The specific criteria for the diagnosis of PTSD for adults is described in the DSM-5.

I have to admit that until this health crisis of mine, I never fully understood my patients' complaints of persistent sleep difficulties following major illness or surgery nor their need for sleeping medication and other tranquilizers. Before my illness, getting to sleep and staying asleep were never a problem. My wife used to tease me that I would be asleep as soon as my head touched the pillow. Following this intense ordeal, I experienced the sleep issues that so many related. It was no longer restful. I often awoke with nightmares, which took months to resolve.

The first step in solving my sleeping issues was my acknowledgment that it was a side effect of my prolonged illness and the distorted sleep that I experienced throughout my hospitalization and rehabilitation. As an in-patient at Spaulding Hospital I had to wear an oxygen saturation monitor and almost every night I set this off when my levels fell. The alarm would ring, and the staff would come charging in to ascertain that I was still breathing. I was still recovering from pneumonia and the ARDS that left my lungs severely damaged so I required nighttime oxygen. I had to sleep on my back, and this position prevents optimal expansion of your lungs when compared to stomach and side sleeping. My preferred sleep position is on my side, but this was not allowed, as my muscle weakness prevented me from changing my body position. This fear of waking up or dying because of disordered breathing became more of a night terror that kept interfering with my experiencing a restful sleep for a long time. An overnight oxygen saturation monitoring test proved that my oxygen levels were satisfactory, and this helped reassure me; however, it took months of cognitive behavioral therapy to help me fully overcome my fear of dying while asleep.

Every sleep expert that I read or spoke with gave me the same advice to overcome this common sleep problem, which they referred to as good sleep hygiene. Going to bed and getting up at the same time even if you are tired is crucial. I was admonished as well against sleeping in on the weekends, as this upsets your circadian sleep clock, which needs to be reset. On the nights that I awoke and was unable to fall back to sleep after twenty or thirty minutes, rather than toss and turn, it was recommended that I get out of bed and read, listen to soothing music, or meditate. It was stressed that a nighttime wind down ritual is very helpful to overcome chronic sleep disturbances.

Avoiding screen time several hours before bed, whether it be cell phone, computer, or television, is important, as it has been repeatedly shown that these activities interfere with sleep onset. The blue light which the screens emit interferes with the body's internal sleep clock. Meditation I found to be very helpful as part of my pre-bedtime ritual, and I found that it has been one of the most successful interventions coupled with the other two listed above. Listening to music helps. I especially found jazz to be beneficial.

High intensity exercise before bedtime should be avoided, as it activates the body's adrenergic system as well as the mind, thus delaying sleep onset. If you find your mind racing, write down a to-do list for the next day. Keep a bedside notebook and pen handy to jot down thoughts that intrude during the time you are falling asleep or if thoughts wake you up.

A hot tub or shower with lavender-scented soap one or two hours before bedtime has been another successful strategy that has strong scientific proof underlying it. When we fall asleep, our body temperature normally drops from a higher to lower level, and a hot bath or shower helps induce this process, as it raises your body temperature prior to entering your bed. It helps to induce sleep onset faster, as our body temperature drops more rapidly from a higher level to the normal sleep zone. Sleeping in a cool room with the windows open or with air conditioning also helps. The evidence for lavender is less scientifically proven, but I also have found it useful when falling asleep was most challenging. Restful sleep occurs more naturally with a calm mind and a body that is clean and cool. Sleep has been shown to be better with a room temperature between 65 to 67 degrees Fahrenheit.

Eating earlier was another useful tactic that I found helpful. It is a lot easier to fall asleep on a stomach that is not full. This also decreases gastroesophageal reflux (GERD) in patients prone to this disorder. GERD is more common as we age and shown to interfere with sleep. We should attempt to finish eating two or three hours before bedtime and avoid pre-bedtime snacks. Caffeine, nicotine, and alcohol should not be consumed several hours before bed. It is not uncommon for people to have several alcoholic beverages with dinner or a night-cap before bed. Although alcohol can often induce sleep onset quickly, it has been scientifically proven to lead to interrupted and less restful sleep. You can do your own experiment on yourself wearing your Apple Watch or similar device to bed and looking at the differences in your heart rate and sleep on nights you imbibe alcohol compared with nights that you avoid alcohol.

I have personally used all of these sleep interventions and have found them to be very effective. They are now part of my pre-bedtime routine. Adopting and customizing my sleep routine took longer than I thought it would and was also harder. It took many months to find the best combination of interventions that worked for me.

My own first episode of intrusion, a hallmark symptom of PTSD, came when a family member was admitted to the ICU with a life-threatening condition. When I visited him in the same Brigham and Women's Hospital ICU where I had been a patient, almost immediately, my heart began to race and a wave of anxiety came over me. I couldn't concentrate and had to excuse myself. I recognized that this was not a normal response. It was following this episode that I first admitted to myself that I may be showing symptoms of PTSD and that I needed to practice self-care. Simply stated, I owed it to myself and my wife to get professional help, which I did.

How did I conquer PTSD? Cognitive behavioral therapy was significantly helpful. Speaking, journaling, acting, and writing are well-validated tools used in this approach, and in a way, this book helped me to successfully overcome my struggle. Much of the story came from the journaling I did during my recovery. Mindfulness meditation is a second established technique that has been demonstrated to effectively treat PTSD symptoms, and both were instrumental to my healing. I read all that I could until I mastered these proven techniques. My life returned to its new normal, but it took time and was not a straight line.

From my and my family's experience, especially when I was on a respirator in the ICU, I do have insight to offer to families impacted similarly from COVID-19. Prior to the virus, those discharged from ICUs with a diagnosis of ARDS commonly experienced depression, anxiety, and symptoms of PTSD, occurring in up to 40 percent of patients or an estimated 1.6 million individuals annually. This number does not include family members affected by the trauma. Those at risk for post COVID-19 PTSD would be an overwhelming number to embrace, as well. Paramount to helping patients and families develop the skills needed to cope is the initiating of counselling while in the hospital. It would have certainly prepared me for mental health issues that were unforeseen and elongated the time necessary for my recovery.

Chapter 14

Posttraumatic Growth

*"You never know how strong you are, until being strong is the
only choice you have."*
Bob Marley

When I returned to work and was still recovering, I
was repeatedly asked two questions. The first was:
Had the lost years spent recovering and the undeniable fact that my life was forever changed made me angry,
bitter? Almost reflexively, I answered no. The second was: Did
the experience make me a better person? This question left me
speechless and unable to easily respond.

Honestly, other than feeling happy to be alive, I had never
considered this possibility. These two questions rattled around
in my head and then they really gnawed at me as the time
needed for recovery and the attendant emotional roller-coaster
dragged on. So, I did what I always do when confronted with
something I didn't know or understand, I researched it.

In 1899, Friedrich Nietzsche said, "That which does not
kill us makes us stronger." A century later, Kelly Clarkson
popularized this observation in her best-selling song "Stronger
(What Doesn't Kill You)." The idea that good can come from
suffering goes back thousands of years, as seen in Judeo-
Christian, Buddhist, Hindu, and ancient Greek writing. One of
the oldest books I read was the Bible, which has many passages
that allude to hardship making you stronger. One verse that

I found particularly true was from Paul in his Letters to the Romans: "We glory in our sufferings, because we know that suffering produces perseverance."

At times this concept seemed more aspirational than real. Another of Nietzsche's observations resonated more deeply: "To live is to suffer, to survive is to find some meaning in the suffering." But as I revisited the books by Frankl, Stockdale, Mandela, Solzhenitsyn, the Bible, and new ones by Hillenbrand and others, I perceived them from a fresh perspective.

My reading on how to recover from near death exposed me to a new concept in psychology, posttraumatic growth (PTG). I was not familiar with this, as it was not taught when I attended college or medical school. First described in 1996 by Richard Tedeschi, Ph.D., PTG is defined as the positive change that occurs as a result of a personal struggle with a life crisis. It is important to differentiate "traumatic, life-altering events" from the day-to-day mild to moderate stresses that help us gain confidence in our abilities and result in wisdom. Those less stressful life experiences build resilience (the ability to recover to one's baseline psychological function). In PTG, the individual not only survives but goes on to experience transformative personal growth that takes one to a higher, previously unknown psychological state. Jennifer King Lindley observed that, "Posttraumatic growth can make us more focused, compassionate and self-aware." However, although PTG is common, it is not guaranteed.

Dr. Tedeschi went on to describe this phenomenon of PTG as having five factors that define major domains. These five areas are part of the Posttraumatic Growth Inventory (PTGI), which is a twenty-one-part assessment tool to help determine a person's progress following trauma:

1. greater appreciation of life,
2. more intimate interpersonal relationships,

3. recognition of new possibilities in life, a new understanding of what is important,

4. a greater sense of personal strength, changed priorities, and

5. a richer existential life with spiritual development.

In *The Posttraumatic Growth Workbook,* Richard Tedeschi and Bret A. Moore articulate a framework to better understand posttraumatic growth and how it interacts with the development of one's life narrative. This breakthrough observation that growth through trauma not only can but does occur was taken a step further when they went on to explain the process and developed treatment programs to help individuals achieve it.

The observation that older and highly educated people tend to demonstrate an easier time processing trauma was speculated to be a consequence of the accumulation of wisdom or life lessons that helped them navigate the trauma. Similarly, posttraumatic growth is seen more profoundly in adolescents and younger adults than in children because it requires an established psychological personality, belief system, position in life, and relationship to be shattered—and these are not present in children. It became clear that I needed to learn how to achieve posttraumatic growth if I was to become the best possible me.

Validation for this observation of PTG was borne out in my readings of the aforementioned life stories of the young adults: Epictetus, Pete Frates, and Louis Zamparelli, as well as those of older men, James Stockdale, Aleksandr Solzhenitsyn, and Nelson Mandela. Thus, we can view posttraumatic growth as a spectrum. Traumas not only upend the individual's life but one's assumptions and dreams of a future life. There is a common devastating realization that, in fact, they are not returning to the life they knew.

One of my greatest fears in life was being paralyzed. When I was a patient on the spinal cord floor at Spaulding

Hospital, the paradox of the profound elation I felt using an electric wheelchair opened up the possibility that from loss, there are unexpected opportunities even when life had been profoundly changed.

Tedeschi and Calhoun go on to state that PTG does not occur as a direct result of the trauma experienced. Rather, it is the survivors' *struggle* with the reality of their new life that is the main component in determining the extent of their growth. Purpose and meaning that existed in their pre-traumatic life are disrupted and need to be restructured. Cognitive behavioral therapy is the psychological technique that can help with rebuilding a new you. PTG is the result of *accepting* the unalterable fact that life as it is now is not what it was. You can't go back or un-ring the bell. This is psychological advanced life support, not first aid, and it is a process that can take years.

In the rereading of my favorite Greek philosopher Epictetus, his journey from injured slave to free man who opens his own school of Stoic philosophy exemplifies PTG. The importance of "choice" in how a person views both the good and bad in one's life experiences is crucial to his teachings. Epictetus acknowledged his disability as part of a broader context of who he was and what his life represented but he did not let his disability define him. In order to illustrate the degree of fame that Epictetus achieved, of note is that the Emperor Marcus Aurelius (credited with guiding the Roman Empire to the apex of its rule) stated in his book *Meditations* that his reading of the lectures of Epictetus were crucial to his intellectual development and leadership. Others are inspired by him to this day.

One book led to another. The next was *Unbroken* by Laura Hillenbrand. This is the riveting story of Louie Zamparelli. With the recounting of his life from childhood to old age, she illustrates what I think are important concepts: resilience (during pre-war and war years), and PTG (in post-war years). We are also presented with an unvarnished, powerful story of the PTSD many veterans suffered upon their return from the war.

Louis was a mischievous boy who by his early teens was well on the way towards juvenile delinquency. He honed his gift for running by escaping from the police. At 14, Louie was failing in school, thereby ineligible for sports and with dim prospects. Pete, his older brother, knew that Louie was craving attention. Petty crime was an easy way to get it, but in the 1930s this was the road to perdition. Pete was a good student and well respected. He met with the high school principal and pleaded for Louie to be allowed to join the track team. This was a pivotal life moment; instead of expulsion, it was discovered that Louie was a natural athlete.

By graduation he had earned 10 varsity letters; however, it was in track that he truly excelled. In 1934 he obliterated the national high school record for the mile. From there Louie went on to the University of Southern California on a track scholarship. As a teenager, he qualified for the 1936 Olympics in the 5,000-meter race and was on the United States of America Olympic track team with Jessie Owens. Louie didn't win but did so well that his coaches felt he had an excellent chance of winning the gold medal at the 1940 Tokyo Olympics, which, unfortunately, were cancelled.

In 1941, Louie joined the Army Air Corps where he was stationed in the Pacific. He survived harrowing combat missions, but ironically, while on a search and rescue mission, his B-24 airplane crash-landed into the shark-infested waters of the Pacific Ocean. The American military search and rescue planes could not find him, but the Japanese did. Japanese fighter planes strafed his life raft but failed to kill him. It was shortly thereafter that he was taken prisoner.

His story of survival for what at the time was an unthinkable number of days spent on a life raft in the open ocean is amazing. (Years later he learned that he and the pilot of his plane set a survival record for the 47 days they spent in a rubber life raft. Lessons learned from their experience went on to change open-water survival training for the United States Military.) The tale of his capture by the Japanese, subsequent torture, and forced slave labor is riveting. It is a well-researched and creditable account of this individual's resilience, built since childhood. What I found most remarkable was what came next.

His life after the war was consumed with anger and unraveled with a descent into alcoholism and despair. His is a heartbreaking story of the PTSD so many returning combat veterans and POWs faced largely alone. He was bitter that his country—the USA—and the Allies never prosecuted Japanese war criminals the way their Nazi counterparts had been held accountable. The sadistic Japanese prison guards who were directly responsible for the starvation, torture, and murder of so many American and ANZAC POWs largely went home unpunished with a free pass. He was bitter that the torture he suffered prevented him from returning to his life's passion of running and made the hope of competing in future Olympics impossible. His life had hit rock bottom from rage and alcoholism. His wife left him, he was unable to work, and he was contemplating suicide when he happened to walk into a tent where the Reverend Billy Graham was speaking. It is not an exaggeration to state that this chance encounter was an epiphany for Louie.

The story that unfolded next is a good example of post-traumatic growth in a young adult. When he exited that tent, he left his corrosive, all-consuming anger at God, at himself, at the sadistic Japanese prison guards, and the world, behind him. Once Zamparelli embraced the healing power of forgiveness, his life became a remarkable story of PTG, which impacted me greatly. It made me feel immensely grateful that I had not succumbed to anger or bitterness following my illness.

There are many components to achieving happiness and resilience in life, but forgiveness is essential. Anger is the road to self-destruction; left unchecked, it can indiscriminately consume everyone near you, whereas forgiveness is the path to healing and happiness. After reading the account of Louie's life, I was totally convinced that posttraumatic growth was a real phenomenon.

My search took me next to identify examples of PTG in older, more educated adults. One that I've already mentioned in Chapter 4 is Admiral James Stockdale. It was during time spent in solitary confinement as a POW that he came to the realization, "I am right where I belong; I am right where I was meant to be." He later went on to say, "Bless you prison, bless you shoot down, bless all the close shaves, all the torture, and all the hairy night landings, and those ready room memories, for having been in my life." He went on to acknowledge that his best insights into human nature were formed behind bars as a POW. His profound perspective on the monumental trauma that he endured exemplifies PTG.

Another PTG inspiration is Aleksandr Solzhenitsyn, born in the Caucasus region a year after the Russian Revolution began. Sadly, his father died in a hunting accident six months before his birth. The family farm was turned into a communist collective, and he was brought up in very humble circumstances by his well-educated mother, who never remarried. She raised him in the Russian Orthodox faith and encouraged his literary and scientific curiosity. At age twelve, despite this upbringing, he joined the Young Pioneers, the Communist Youth Organization where atheism was espoused and religion expunged.

After marrying in 1940, Solzhenitsyn went on to graduate from Rostov State University in 1941, where he excelled in mathematics and physics. He found that writing interested him and in his spare time took correspondence courses from the Moscow Institute of Philosophy, Literature, and History. Following graduation, he joined the Red Army, rose to the rank of captain, and went on to become a commander of an artillery brigade. He saw heavy combat on the Russian front, then later in Germany. The raw, unvarnished horror of war was experienced firsthand. He witnessed atrocities perpetrated on the Russian people by the German Army and later by the Russian Army on German civilians. He won decorations on two occasions and was also awarded the Order of the Red Star.

After the war, on February of 1945, Solzhenitsyn was arrested in Germany by agents of the Soviet Agency SMERSH (a term coined by Joseph Stalin. It was an umbrella organization for three counter-intelligence agencies in the Red Army) for writing anti-Soviet propaganda. The charges were based on a letter that he wrote to a school friend in which he not only criticized but ridiculed Stalin. After interrogation in Moscow's feared Lubyanka prison, he was sentenced to eight years in a slave labor camp. The horror of life in the Gulag went well beyond what he had experienced during the war years. Fellow Russians were brutalized, starved, exploited, and worked to death in sub-zero cold.

After Solzhenitsyn finished his prison term, he was sentenced to life in exile. In 1956, his punishment had him teaching high school physics and astronomy in a remote region of Kazakhstan. In 1962, his first book, *One Day in the Life of Ivan Denisovich*, was published, due to the personal intervention of Nikita Khrushchev, who wanted Stalin's crimes against humanity and against his fellow Russians exposed. Other books followed, and in 1970 he won the Nobel Prize in Literature "…for the ethical force with which he pursued the indispensable traditions of Russian literature." On August 8, 1971, the KGB allegedly tried to assassinate him with the chemical ricin.

His opus was the 1973 epic, three-volume, seven-part *Gulag Archipelago* in which he detailed the endless nightmare life imposed by the Stalin regime on what he calculated to be close to 60 million Russian civilians, including men, women, and children. The existence of the Gulag prisons had been rumored, but he was the first to expose the state-sponsored terrorism. The book is based on his imprisonment from 1945 to 1953, the testimony of 256 former Gulag prisoners and exhaustive research into the Russian Communist penal system. For writing this book (never published in the Soviet Union), he was arrested once again in 1974, stripped of his Soviet citizenship, and deported to West Germany.

The war years demonstrate Solzhenitsyn's resiliency, but it was the eight years spent as a prisoner and the years that followed that I believe demonstrate that he met the criteria for posttraumatic growth. In a powerfully moving passage in "The Ascent," one of the final chapters in Volume 2 of the *Gulag Archipelago*, he reflects on when he "…lay there on the rotting prison straw that I sensed within myself the first stirrings of good. Gradually it was disclosed that the line separating good and evil passes not between the states nor between classes nor between political parties but right through all human hearts. And that is why I turn my back to the years of my imprisonment and say, sometimes to the astonishment of those about me, bless you prison, for having been in my life." In this same chapter, he goes on to talk about his realization that you must risk your life to help others or, said differently, the need to be "your brother's keeper."

When asked to summarize the cause of this disastrous period, he stated, "Men have forgotten God; that's why this has happened." Despite the years of crushing savagery that he was subjected to, psychologically he did not break. He found meaning and purpose in exposing the horror of the Gulag system.

Of course, I must highlight Nelson Mandela as representing my final example of posttraumatic growth. In reading his life story, it is my opinion that at some point during his imprisonment, he moved from resilience to posttraumatic growth. He transformed from a revolutionary freedom fighter committed to violence into one of the world's greatest leaders, akin to Mahatma Gandhi and Martin Luther King, espousing non-violent change.

Despite 27 years of imprisonment, hard labor, and extreme deprivation beyond what even the most violent prisoners were forced to endure, he was not crushed as a human being. My conclusion is that his age, education, and cumulative life experience protected him from being shattered as a younger person may have been. Time incarcerated helped shape his spiritual development. Mandela exited prison with a deep understanding of the immense power that forgiveness brings, which is essential for both healing and happiness.

In a 1975 letter to his wife Winnie, he wrote, "Honesty, sincerity, simplicity, humility, pure generosity, absence of vanity, readiness to serve others—qualities which are within easy reach of every soul—are the foundations of one's spiritual life." Prison revealed the critical importance of service to others as a foundation of one's life. He envisioned peace and reconciliation, not violence and retribution as the preferred path for his country.

Following intense international pressure, he was eventually released from prison in 1990 at age 72. Several months later, he offered a ceasefire to the ruling Afrikaners who found him surprisingly moderate. This concession outraged many of his more militant countrymen, including his wife, who had also fought against apartheid and had suffered as had he. Despite this opposition, he prevailed and in 1991 was elected President of the ANC. Later in 1991, he was elected President of South Africa.

Many feared he would seek revenge for the atrocities suffered under Afrikaner rule, but he did not. He met with members of the losing apartheid regime. He stated that, "Courageous people do not fear forgiving, for the sake of peace." The 1995 Rugby World Cup was held in South Africa, and he urged all of South Africa to come together and cheer for the national team. It was a momentous time of healing for the South Africans, cheering for their team as a united nation. South Africa went on to defeat the always fearsome team from New Zealand and won the 1995 Rugby World Cup.

Mandela appointed Desmond Tutu as the chair of the Truth and Reconciliation Commission to investigate crimes committed by the apartheid regime and also by the ANC. The commission granted individual amnesty in return for testimony. He said the findings of the commission "helped us move away from the past to concentrate on the present and future," and went on to give us many lessons to live by such as: "Like slavery and apartheid, poverty is not natural. It is man-made and can be overcome and eradicated by the actions of human beings." "No one is born hating another person because of the color of his skin, his background, or his religion. People must learn to hate, and if they can learn to hate, they can be taught to love, for love comes more naturally to the human heart than its opposite," and "There can be no greater gift than that of giving one's time and energy to help others without expecting anything in return." Nelson Mandela emerged from prison not embittered but as his "brother's keeper." He went on to win the Nobel Peace Prize and changed the world for the better.

I am not equating myself with these men of grand stature, but I have been greatly inspired by them to rise above the intensely painful challenges presented in my own humble life. And in doing so, firmly believe that everyone else has this opportunity for growth and healing as well. As a result of my illness, there was no doubt that I had a better appreciation of life and of things that I had previously taken for granted, the simplest being walking and breathing. Mindfulness training had taught me to be more fully present with myself, my family, and friends. Hence, I enjoyed more intimate and intense relationships with them, many who had also been changed by their experience of what I went through. It can't be underestimated how life altering this type of shared situation is on anyone who loves you.

My entire professional life was spent becoming the best doctor possible through hard work and self-sacrifice. I was, by all measures, a very successful physician. Gratefully, I recognized that the mindfulness training I had learned for my own recovery also helped me to better care for patients entrusted to my care. I was more fully present with them. It is ironic that becoming a patient, dangerously close to death, had helped me become a better physician. Instead of listening to my patients with compassion, I listened empathetically because I, too, had experienced what it felt like to endure a serious illness and a long and incomplete recovery. My life narrative had changed. Empathy was no longer just a word in the dictionary; I knew what it was like to be a patient. It was not something that I had tried to accomplish. It is not an exam you can study for.

What made me a better person was the quite random event of being a patient and nearly dying twice. The world that I had known transformed. Even though my life was indelibly altered, I was more profoundly aware of what was important to me. My priorities came sharply into focus and slowly, new possibilities presented themselves, such as writing this book. Paradoxically, even though my body was weaker, I had more confidence in my inner strength and what I could overcome. I evolved because of what I had endured. The realization that I was not invincible and that my time was limited did not frighten me. Quite the opposite happened, in that I learned to thrive and became more fully alive.

My faith expanded in tandem. It had been a part of my life since childhood, yet as an adult, faith was not something I spent much time dwelling on. Formed when I was young, it remained in the background through most of my life. After my medical crisis, it felt quite different. The undercurrent of the fear of doing something wrong was no longer there. Faith felt more spiritual, more real, and more like an adult rather than a child-like faith.

Life provides numerous opportunities to become the best version of ourselves possible but only if we allow our experiences to let us grow. Sometimes this comes unconsciously, like osmosis, and other times it calls for effort. In essence, these life lessons help us form a moral and ethical compass that guides us. At other times, the challenges, trials and tribulations of life cause us to lose our bearings. When this happens, we must take the time to assess where we are, where we came from, and where we want to go. This active process requires introspection and time. There are usually multiple paths. If our choices are made with respect for our fellow man and in service to others, the path is just. We have that opportunity to fulfil our highest potential at each stage of life, with each challenge faced and milestone reached. It is imperative to make proper use of these moments.

Continuous quality improvement is a highly regarded business management practice pioneered by W. Edward Deming. Continuous improvement is a never-ending process with a goal of increasing the efficiency in any organization or human endeavor. My experience has led me to believe that this concept of continuous improvement is applicable to all of mankind at all stages of life, not solely business management. As humans, we should constantly strive to improve. Throughout life, we have the capacity for self-improvement by commitment to life-long learning, love, and practicing forgiveness of both self and others. Non-judgmental self-compassion is essential for happiness.

The answer to the question that I was asked is yes, the searing experiences of these past years did in fact help make me a better person.

Epilogue

I started writing this book in the winter of 2020 when COVID-19 began to ravage the world. Currently, in 2024, the world remains at war with the virus. What have we learned? The human race will survive. Despite this back-to-back "Annus Horribilis" caused by COVID 19, viral illness and pneumonia are not new nor are pandemics. COVID will become endemic such as influenza and other respiratory viruses that we coexist with.

We did, however, underestimate this virus. The death toll, terrifying during the winter of 2020, has grown to a previously unthinkable number. As of the completion of this book, there have been 625,796,026 confirmed cases of COVID-19 and 6,558,493 deaths worldwide, most likely an undercount due to limited and unequal testing at the pandemic's onset. The number of infected and dead increases daily. At the onset of the epidemic this virus didn't follow the usual seasonal variations. It was a 365-day public-health menace. As time passed the virus reverted to the seasonal pattern observed with usual respiratory pathogens. Newer viral strains were highly transmissible though less lethal and given enough time will leave few people free of a COVID-19 infection.

This has led to a lifestyle bifurcation of the population with the young and otherwise healthy resuming their pre-pandemic lives, eschewing masks and social isolation. However, it is crucial that adequate resources to protect our most vulnerable (those older or younger but with co-morbidities) are available and easily accessed to prevent unnecessary hospital admissions and death. As a nation, we can't afford the return to field hospitals and cancellation of elective procedures so that staff can be redeployed to care for those critically ill from COVID-19. As a physician, I'm concerned with how our healthcare system continues to be maximally stressed and would be seriously challenged if forced to handle the surges seen in the winter of 2020 and 2021.

The massive demand for medical care caused by the pandemic has led to an unprecedented nationwide depletion of health care providers, estimated to be as high as 20 percent. We have gone from a dearth of personal protective equipment to a shortage of medical staff. This is no longer a supply chain problem but one with more far-reaching consequences. And shocking, too, is the rise in verbal and physical abuse these healthcare workers have been and continue to be subjected to. This unacceptable problem is being poorly addressed and continues to rise. The ongoing moral injury endured by these healthcare providers will have its reckoning.

Physicians, nurses and for that matter all health care providers choose their profession to fulfill a personal need to help others. Their job gives them mission and purpose but can lead to chronic unhappiness for reasons cited below. The work is hard, often involving rotations between day, evening, and nights shifts. Patient care is 24/7. This disruption to the normal diurnal pattern is unhealthy. Working on the in-patient side, providers often perform their jobs understaffed and under supplied. Medications, equipment, and other supplies are not always available. This leads to unnecessary stress when providers are asked to complete their jobs without adequate support. They do the best that they can with what they have, but the choices are difficult when they can't care for the patients the way that would be considered best practice. Nurses and physicians face verbal and physical assault in the emergency rooms and on the floors by patients, their family members, and friends. Hospitals now have security and police presence around the clock to help, but their intervention only occurs when the situation escalates to a dangerous level. There can be no joy with this "just getting by," knowing that their work conditions make doing their job a tenuous exercise. This real-life problem eats away like a parasite the joy that your job of caring for others should bring. Instead it results in repetitive moral injury.

On the outpatient side of health care the challenges of doing a good job overlap that of the inpatient. There are not enough providers to expeditiously care for existing patients, necessitating the use of emergency rooms to fill the void. The Center for Medicare Services (CMS) refers to this problem as avoidable emergency room admissions. Access issues are a crucial problem with no simple solution. Large groups and for-profit entities have built urgent care facilities to help fill the need, but these are insufficient. New patients often have to wait months to see their chosen primary care physician. Access is a huge problem. There are simply not enough physicians and advanced practice providers (APPs) available to meet the growing need.

When patients are evaluated and found by their physician to need imaging studies, referrals, or new medications, it is not unusual to hit a wall where physicians are asked to call the insurance company and get prior authorization. Also it is not unusual to have the request denied by a non-physician at which point you give up or go through an appeals process to advocate for your patient, a process that can take days to weeks and consume hours of time. This requires taking time out of a busy schedule that has no free time set aside so you can advocate on your patient's behalf with one of the insurance company physicians. Other hurdles are when a patient has an acute or chronic illness that needs an evidenced-based medication that the insurance company will not cover or will cover but with an enormous co-pay. When the patient tells you that they can't afford the indicated medication, then you have to try to come up with a less-than-optimal substitute at a cost that the patient can live with. These repeated scenarios lead to moral injury that chips away at even the most resolute physician or nurse. It is no surprise then to know that up to 20 percent of nurses and physicians are contemplating leaving their professions for some other job or choosing early retirement.

Chronic underinvestment in nursing schools, medical schools, and training programs for medical/surgical/psychiatric physicians will take decades to remediate. This is reflected in what has become a chronic overcrowding problem for emergency rooms. It is not unusual to find patients lying on stretchers lining every inch of hallway space. Patients can wait for days to get a hospital bed. Some patients *never* get a bed prior to discharge. From my own personal experience, I know this to be true. In 2022, I was hospitalized three times, twice for pneumonia and once for acute appendicitis. I spent the entirety of the first two admissions in the emergency room and that last in the post-acute-surgical care recovery unit from which I was discharged. There were no inpatient beds available.

Sadly, familiarity with death is an unpleasant part of most jobs in healthcare. Death from COVID-19 has been far in excess of what would be seen during a lifetime career in healthcare. What these heroes went through and continue to go through is not normal. The emotional and physical toll on the healthcare community of our nation is a burden that they have unselfishly shouldered but at tremendous personal cost. In multiple instances of above-and-beyond compassion, medical staff volunteered their personal time off to sit with patients so that they would not die alone. Alas, some healthcare workers died in the line of duty caring for those stricken. My respect is immense for the providers of these selfless acts of caring and courage.

It is disheartening to learn that alcohol consumption is up nationally since the start of the pandemic, as are overdoses from opioids. Violent crime such as murder has also spiked. These findings highlight the red-flag warning of maladaptive behavior manifesting as a consequence of the ongoing trauma and isolation caused by the pandemic. This will potentially be a catastrophe but with more long-term consequences to society than the pandemic. The world may be even less prepared for this crisis than it was for COVID-19.

Yet I remain hopeful. Perhaps it's due to my religious and spiritual life, or maybe I can attribute this to living long enough to understand society's ability to rise from the ashes again and again. We can work together. Just as in the race to place a man on the moon, scientists and the private sector, with the help of government funding, cooperated to bring from concept to reality, vaccines and monoclonal antibodies to treat the virus at unimaginable speed. In a recent article in *Lancet Infectious Diseases,* it is estimated that 19,800,000 lives have been saved from COVID-19 vaccines worldwide. The Imperial College of London estimates that vaccinations decrease the death rate by 63 percent. Of course, there are risks that need to be discussed regarding vaccines, for medication, or any procedure, but they are miniscule in comparison to the benefits. My view is that adverse events can be minimized if informed consent is discussed prior to vaccination.

On another positive note, knowledge and innovation were widely shared. For instance, placing patients in a prone position to improve their breathing was not new and is remarkable in its simplicity. However, the magnitude of patients needing repositioning led to formalized rapid response teams to overcome the logistics needed to turn them. Likewise, for patients with mandated respiratory precautions, the idea of using cell phones, tablets, and computers helped ease their isolation and need for human interaction with loved ones.

Our world is interdependent. Cross-global knowledge facilitates new vaccines and therapies. Recently developed anti-viral therapeutic medications have been found to effectively treat COVID-19 outpatients with early stages of the illness, thus improving survival and lessening the need for hospitalization. In addition, other medications have been approved and some are pending emergency use authorization (EUA) by the FDA and the European Medicines Agency Task Force to treat hospitalized patients requiring oxygen and at high risk for a life-threatening cytokine storm, ARDS.

The ability to Acknowledge, Accept, and Adapt, will help anyone survive even the unimaginable. This is what helped me at every stage of my illness and recovery in 2014 and supported my return to a life more enriched than before. It helps me now in my current battle with cancer, which has forced me to give up patient care in order to better care for myself. Life offers up waves of health and sickness, challenges, and achievements. I hope my story of healing will inspire you to, in my father's words, "Never give up."

Afterword
A Wife's Perspective

We have never been fancy New Year's Eve people, choosing instead to celebrate with family and friends. Our plan for 2014 was a small house gathering; our sons would be traveling down to New York City to ring in the New Year with friends. Although Michael had been battling a terrible cold and congestion for two weeks, the night of December 31 was like he fell off a cliff. Calling 911, waiting that eternity for the ambulance to transport him to the hospital where he was on staff, began what can only be described as a complete nightmare. So much comes to mind from that night…

Arriving in the ER, I saw my husband truly struggling for his life, for every breath. I knew, as a nurse myself with years of ICU experience, that this could not be sustained. Calls went out first to our sons. I was unable to reach our older son and instructed our youngest to keep trying him, that they needed to come right away. I prayed they would get to the hospital in time. The remaining calls were a blur—to Michael's and my family—asking them to pass along the information to each other.

Hospital staff worked quickly to try to stabilize him. These were many of the same people we had socialized with at various events. Since they knew me and of my training, I was kept informed of every chest X-ray, lab result, medication ordered, and specialist consulted. Being able to stay in "nurse mode" instead of "wife" helped me to control the terrifying fear that I would lose my husband that night.

Michael was transferred to the ICU, where it was clear, based on how hard he was working to breathe and his deteriorating oxygen levels, that he would need to be intubated. I explained to him that this would be better if done electively, knowing that if he abruptly decompensated, it would be far more traumatic. Although I completely understood how precarious the situation was, it was driven home even more so by one of his physician colleagues who had been consulted. This caring doctor tried his best to describe how ill Michael was, and while showing me his chest X-ray, broke down in tears. The strain on the staff was tremendous and palpable.

The decision was made to transfer him to another Boston hospital with the ability to offer more support for lungs that were so damaged, they were unable to allow oxygen to flow into his system. Only a small window was open for this transfer due to an impeding snowstorm. I felt like it was a good omen when the MediVac ground team of three arrived—all named Michael.

You have read in Michael's story the details of his experience that he can recall. For family members, watching your loved one suffer is a special kind of hell. It is understood in the medical community how much a part of a patient's recovery is shaped by the support and love of family and close friends. So, what might my perspective offer to others facing this type of life changing event? I can best speak to what helped me personally.

Communication is key. Although I was in a unique situation, you, too, can receive information on your loved one's health status. My nursing training and work experience were extremely helpful. Being privy to the details—and understanding what they meant—allowed me to process not only where things stood but also helped me let family members know. How many of us have been to a medical appointment and felt that there was an entirely different language being spoken? It's okay to ask for clarification on terms, plans of care, etcetera, in order to understand and be an active participant. The ICU nurses were so very kind to me, as I'm sure I was a pain in the neck! They patiently gave me the information I craved to keep myself from falling apart emotionally. The doctors spoke frankly and clearly about the plan for the day and did seem to value my input. It works best to have one family member be the main contact person, as it's unreasonable to ask hospital staff to keep repeating information and this takes them away from time with other patients and families. While I would personally speak with our sons, it was helpful to have a couple of family members or friends share in dispensing information. Emails are helpful too, but at the end of a very long and exhausting day, they are somewhat burdensome.

Communicating with your loved one who is ill is also necessary. Tuning in to how they may be feeling is something that you may be more adept at recognizing—especially if they cannot speak. Thankfully, I could tell that Mike was in pain due to being positioned on his bad hip and was able to advocate for him.

Take care of yourself. This is so hard when the beloved patient is having a hard time. I have always been happy to offer a helping hand where needed, but honestly, not very good at accepting help myself. With the length of time and severity of Michael's condition, I realized how much I needed the love and support of friends and family. The hospital allowed a family member to sleep overnight in the room (in a chair), or in the waiting area while he was critical. Although I felt I needed to be there, I was comforted knowing that a loved one could spell me off and allow me to go home, shower, and rest in my own bed. Friends brought food, knowing if I had to actually cook something, it would probably not happen. They watched out for our sons, calling and checking in with them to offer love and emotional support (and even helped with plane reservations). I became aware that people who cared about me knew that they could not change what was going on, but they did what Mother Teresa used to speak about: "small things with great love." I accepted their love with grace.

This brings me to the power of prayer. In those critical days, I asked everyone I knew to start a prayer chain and to reach out to their friends and family, far and wide, regardless of faith or religion. I embraced the statement, "There are no atheists in foxholes," and felt the desperate need for God's help. A friend told me that she really didn't believe in God but she prayed anyway just to try to help. And did it? My belief system tells me it did. When I met up with one of the doctors who saw Michael that first night, he told me Michael had been the only one of four patients they saw that week, with the same diagnosis, that survived.

Remember to pace yourself. This harkens back to taking care of yourself, but what I'm really addressing is for the long term. When caring for someone with acute illness, you seem to get by on little sleep, terrible food choices, and adrenalin. That truly becomes unsustainable as time moves on. Long days in the ICU followed by the transfer to rehab was the continuation of an arduous journey. Although I was able to be present most of the time, there were days when I could not. Snowy weather that made driving treacherous gave me permission to take a day off, even if just to pay the bills, do some laundry, and clean my house. Also, instead of being there 12-plus hours, sometimes I'd cut back and have friends or family visit Michael.

Be grateful. I feel a tremendous sense of gratitude. For our sons, who in addition to all of their help with their father, showed me what mature, wonderful, and loving men they are. For our family members who stepped up big time to be there to support us. I had them so well trained; they knew when they visited that they'd need to be able to report vital signs to me so I'd know how things were going. For the hospital staff: doctors, nurses, respiratory and physical therapists, cleaning staff, etcetera, who were so professional, competent, and caring. For my friends, who have continued on this journey with me over the years. For their offers of love and support and the ability to know that sometimes the best that can be said is "that sucks." But the person I am most grateful for is Michael, my dear husband. How many times when it seemed all was dire, you fought your way back to me. You continue to show your strength and courage every day, trying to face challenges head on. You inspire me to try my best every day.

Resources

Suggested Reading, Viewing, and Listening

Prologue

Soderbergh, Steven. *Contagion*. 2011. United States: Warner Bros.

Chapter 1 - The Light

Sommers, Stephen. *The Mummy Returns*. 2001. Universal City, CA: Alphaville Films.

Chapter 2 - I Can Hear You

McKegney, F. P. "The Intensive Care Syndrome: The Definition, Treatment, and Prevention of a New 'Disease of Medical Progress.'" *Connecticut Medicine* 30, no.9 (1966): 633-6.

Chapter 3 - Staying Sane

Carlson, Rachel. *Silent Spring* (New York: Houghton Mifflin, 1962).

Crosby, Donald F. *Battlefield Chaplains: Catholic Priests in World War II* (Lawrence: University Press of Kansas, 1994), 26.

Dumas, Alexander. *The Count of Monte Cristo*. (London: Penguin Classics, 2003).

Epictetus. *Enchiridion* (Mineola: Dover Publications, Inc., 2004).

Frankl, Victor. *Man's Search for Meaning* (Boston: Beacon Press, 2006).

Frost, Robert. "Stopping by the Woods on a Snowy Evening" in *The Poetry of Robert Frost.* (Henry Holt and Company, LLC, 1923).

Stockdale, James. *Thoughts of a Philosophical Fighter Pilot* (Stanford: Hoover Press, 1995).

Plum, Fred and Posner, Jerome. *Diagnosis of Stupor and Coma.* (Oxford University Press, 2007).

Poe, Edgar Allen. *Cask of Amontillado.*

Poe, Edgar Allen. *Fall of the House of Usher.*

Saint Jude Thaddeus. stjudeleague@claretians.org.

Chapter 4 - Find Your Strength

Collins, Jim. *Good to Great: Why Some Companies Make the Leap and Others Don't.* (New York: Harper Business, 2001)

Dancing with the Stars. ABC Television.

Frankl, Victor. *Man's Search for Meaning* (Boston: Beacon Press, 2006).

Zemeckis, Robert. *Forrest Gump.* 1994. United States: Paramount Pictures.

Chapter 5 - How Could This Happen?

1901 Nobel Prize in Physiology (Medicine), Emil von Behring.

Resources

American Thoracic Society. "Top 20 Pneumonia Facts—2019." https://www.thoracic.org/patients/patient-resources/resources/top-pneumonia-facts.pdf. Accessed June 13, 2024.

Artigas, A. Bernard, G.R., Carlet, J., Dreyfuss, D., Gattinoni, L., Hudson, L., Lamy, M., Marini, J. J., Matthay, M.A., Pinsky, M.R., et al. "The American-European Consensus Conference on ARDS, Part 2. Ventilatory, Pharmacologic, Supportive Therapy, Study Design Strategies and Issues Related to Recovery and Remodeling. Acute Respiratory Distress Syndrome." *American Journal of Respiratory and Critical Care Medicine* 157, no.4 pt. 1 (April 1998): 1332-47.

Ashbaugh, D.G., Bigelow, D.B., Petty, T.L., and Levine, B.E. "Acute Respiratory Distress in Adults." *The Lancet* 2, no. 7511. (August 1967): 319.

Bellani, G., Laffet, C.S., Paul, D.W., et al. "Epidemiology, Patterns of Care, and Mortality for Patients with Acute Respiratory Distress Syndrome in Intensive Care Units in 50 Countries." *JAMA* 315, vol.8 (February 2016): 788-800.

Eccles, Ron. "Understanding the Symptoms of the Common Cold and Influenza." *The Lancet Infectious Diseases* 5, no. 11 (November 2005): 718-25.

Heikkinen, Tehro and Järvinen, Asko. "The Common Cold." *The Lancet* 361, no. 9351 (January 2003): 51-9.

Johnstone, Jennie, Majumdar, Sumit R., Fox, Julie D., and Marrie, Thomas J. "Viral Infection in Adults Hospitalized with Community Acquired Pneumonia: Prevalence, Pathogens and Presentation." *Chest* 134, no.6 (December 2008): 1141-8.

Kirkpatrick, G. L. "The Common Cold." *Primary Care* 23, no.4 (December 1996): 657.

Kwok, Yen Lee Angela, Gralton, Jan, and McLaws, Mary-Louise. "Face Touching: A Frequent Habit That Has Implications for Hand Hygiene." *American Journal of Infection Control* 43, no.2 (February 2015):112-114.

Lister, J. "On a New Method of Treating Compound Fractures, Abscess, etc." *The Lancet* 90, no. 2291 (1867): 91-120.

Mikkelsen, M.E., Netzer, G., and Iwashyna T. UpToDate. "Post-Intensive Care Syndrome." October 4, 2015.

Pasteur, Louis. "Memoire sur la Fermentation Appele e Lactique." *Comptes Rendu Hebdomadaires des Seances de l'Academie des Sciences* 45 (1857): 913-916.

Ralby A. "The Crimean War 1853-1856." *Atlas of Military History*. (Parragon, 2013).

Turner, R.B. "Epidemiology, Pathogenesis and Treatment of the Common Cold." *Annals of Allergy, Asthma & Immunology* 78, no.6 (June 1997): 531.

Ramirez, J. A. UpToDate. "Overview of Community Acquired Pneumonia in Adults. March 13, 2020.

Siegel, M. D. UpToDate. "Acute Respiratory Distress Syndrome: Prognosis and Outcomes in Adults." March 6, 2017.

Wang, Chen Y., Calfee, Carolyn S., Paul, Devon W., Janz, David R., May, Addison K., Zhou, Hanjing, Bernard, Gordon R., Matthay, Michael A., et al. "One-year Mortality and Predictors of Death Among Hospital Survivors of Acute

Respiratory Distress Syndrome." *Intensive Care Medicine* 40, no. 3 (March 2014): 388-96.

Chapter 6 - Jesuit Education

Doidge, Norman. *The Brain That Changes Itself: Stories of Personal Triumph from the Frontiers of Brain Science.* (New York: Penguin, 2007).

Ericsson, K., Krampe, R.T., and Tesch-Römer, C. "The Role of Deliberate Practice in the Acquisition of Expert Performance." *Psychological Review* 100, no. 3 (1993): 363-406.

Mandela, Nelson. "Excerpt from a Speech Given in South Africa on July 16, 2003 Commemorating the Launch of Mindset Network."

Ratio Studiorum (Ratio atque Institutio Studiorum Societas jesu). 1598; revised 1832.

Stockdale, James. *Thoughts of a Philosophical Fighter Pilot.* (Stanford: Hoover Press, 1995).

Wessling, Henry J. "S.J. Bulletin of the American Association of Jesuit Scientists." May 1, 1947.

Chapter 7 - The Long Road

Geisel, Theodor Seuss. *Oh the Places You'll Go.* (New York: Random House, 1990).

Huddleston, Peggy. *Prepare for Surgery, Heal Faster: A Guide of Mind-Body Techniques.* (Cambridge: Angel River Press, 2005).

Niebuhr, Reinhold. *The Essential Reinhold Niebuhr: Selected Essays and Addresses.* (New Haven: Yale University Press, 1986).

Nietzsche, Friedrich. *Twilight of the Idols, or, How to Philosophize with a Hammer 1899* (Penguin Classics, 1990).

Spielberg, Steven. *Saving Private Ryan.* 1998. United States: DreamWorks, Paramount Pictures.

Chapter 8 - Pain

Barron, Zach. "George Clooney When We Need Him Most." *GQ,* November 17, 2020.

Coyne, Karin S., Margolis, Mary Kay, Yeomans, Karen, King, Frederic R., Chavoshi, Soheil, Payne, Krista A., and Casale, Robert J., "Opioid-Induced Constipation Among Patients with Chronic Noncancer Pain in the United States, Canada, Germany, and the United Kingdom; Laxative Use, Response, and Symptom Burden Over Time." *Pain Medicine* 16, no.8 (August 2015):1551-65.

"Diverticulosis." *Stedman's Medical Dictionary.*

Grastontechnique.com. Accessed June 13, 2024.

Huddleson, Peggy. *Huddleston's Relaxation/Healing CD Plus Instructional CD.* (Cambridge: Angel River Press, 2005).

Huddleston, Peggy. *Prepare for Surgery, Heal Faster: A Guide of Mind-Body Techniques.* (Cambridge: Angel River Press, 2005).

Lee, Marion, Silverman, Sanford M., Hansen, Hans, Patel, Vikram B. and Manchikanti, Laxmaiah. "A Comprehensive

Review of Opioid-Induced Hyperalgesia. *Pain Physician* 14, no.2, (March – April 2011):145-161.

Max, M. B. "Improving Outcomes of Analgesic Treatment: Is Education Enough?" *Annals of Internal Medicine* 113, no.13 (December 1, 1990): 885-9.

Physician's Desk Reference. 2020.

Webster, Lynn R. and Webster, Rebecca M. "Predicting Aberrant Behaviors in Opioid-Treated Patients: Preliminary Validation of the Opioid Risk Tool." *Pain Medicine* 6, no. 6 (November – December 2005): 432.

Chapter 9 – Meditation

Brown, D. *Meditation for Peak Performance and Everyday Living.* Harvard Medical School.

Butler, D. "Understanding Pain in 5 Minutes and What to Do About It."

Di Liegro, Carlo Maria, Schiera, Gabriella, Proia, Patrizia, and Di Liegro, Italia. "Physical Activity and Brain Health." *Genes (Basel)* 10, no.9 (September 2019): 720.

Everyday Health. www.everydayhealth.com. Accessed June 13, 2024.

Kabat-Zinn, Jon. *Full Catastrophe Living: Using the Wisdom of Your Body and Mind to Face Stress, Pain and Illness* (Delta Trade Paperbacks, 1991).

Kral, Tammi RA, Schuyler, Brianna S. Mumford, Jeanette A., Rosenkranz, Melissa A, Lutz, Antoine and Davidson,

Richard J. "Impact of Short- and Long-Term Mindfulness Meditation Training on Amygdala Reactivity to Emotional Stimuli." *Neuroimage* 181 (November 2018): 301-313.

Huddleston, Peggy. *Prepare for Surgery, Heal Faster: A Guide of Mind-Body Techniques.* (Cambridge: Angel River Press, 2005).

Mokhari, Tahmineh, Tu, Yiheng and Hu, Li. "Involvement of the Hippocampus in Chronic Pain and Depression." *Brain Science Advances* 5, no.4 (2019): 288-98.

Neugebauer, Volker. "Amygdala Pain Mechanisms." *The Handbook of Experimental Pharmacology* 227 (2015): 261-284.

Saint Ignatius of Loyola. *Spiritual Exercises.*

Tauben D. and Stacey B. R. UpToDate. "Approach to the Management of Chronic Non-Cancer Pain in Adults." Nov 20, 2020.

Chapter 10 - Resilience

Bhalla, Nita. Reuters. "Mandela Calls for Gandhi's Non-Violence Approach." January 29, 2007. https://www.reuters.com/article/idUSDEL342197/.

Brand, Christo. *Doing Life with Mandela: My Prisoner, My Friend* (United Kingdom: John Blake Publishing, 2014).

Brown, Daniel James. *The Boys in the Boat.* (Penguin Books, June 4, 2013).

Coutu, Diane L. "How Resilience Works" *Harvard Business Review* 80, no.5 (May 2002): 46-50, 52, 55.

Duckworth, Angela. *Grit: The Power of Passion and Perseverance.* (Scribner, May 2016).

Frankl, Victor. *Man's Search for Meaning* (Boston: Beacon Press, 2006).

Hillenbrand, Laura. *Seabiscuit: An American Legend* (Random House, 2001).

Mandela, Nelson. *Long Walk to Freedom: The Autobiography of Nelson Mandela* (Little Brown & Co, 1994).

Oxford Living Dictionary.

Schiraldi, Glen R. *The Resilience Workbook: Essential Skill to Recover from Stress, Trauma and Adversity.* (New Harbinger Publications, November 2017).

Vaillant, George. "Grant Study of 268 Harvard College Graduates."

Wicks, Robert J. *Bounce: Living the Resilient Life* (Oxford University Press, 2010).

Wicks, Robert J. *Perspective: The Calm Within the Storm* (Oxford University Press, 2014).

Wicks, Robert J. www.robertjwicks.com. Accessed June 13, 2024.

Chapter II - Life's Purpose and Meaning

1952 Nobel Peace Prize, Albert Schweitzer.

Alimujiang, Aliya, Wiensch, Ashley, Boss, Jonathan, Fleischer, Nancy L., Mondul, Alison M., McLean, Karen, Mukherjee,

Bhramar and Pearce, Celeste Leigh. "Association Between Life Purpose and Mortality Among US Adults Older than 50 Years." *JAMA Network Open* 2, no.5 (May 2019): e194270.

Aristotle. *Eudemian Ethics*

Arrian. *Enchiridion* (Mineola: Dover Publications, Inc.): 2004.

Cousins, Norman. *Anatomy of an Illness as Perceived by the Patient* (New York: W.W. Norton & Company, 1979).

Dumas, Alexandre. *The Count of Monte Cristo* (Penguin Classics, 2003).

Einstein, Albert. *New York Times*, June 20, 1932.

Epictetus. *Discourses and Selected Writings* (London: Penguin Classics, 2008).

Frankl, Victor. *Man's Search for Meaning* (Boston: Beacon Press, 2006).

Garcia, Hector and Miralles, Francesco. *Ikigai* (Penguin Books, 2016).

Jung, Carl. *Modern Man in Search of Soul* (London: Routledge & Kegan Paul, 1933).

Merton, Thomas. *No Man is an Island* (Barnes & Noble Books, 2003).

Merton, Thomas. *The Seven Story Mountain* (Harcourt, October 11, 1948).

National Book Review. "The 100 Best Non-Fiction Books of the Century." May 3, 1999.

Sherman, Casey and Wedge, Dave. *The Ice Bucket Challenge: Pete Frates and the Fight Against ALS* (Fore Edge, September 5, 2017).

Smith, Emily Esfahanin. "Meaning Is Healthier than Happiness." *The Atlantic.* August 1, 2013. https://www. theatlantic.com/health/archive/2013/08/meaning-is-healthier-than-happiness/278250/.

Chapter 12 - Happiness

Aquinas, Thomas. *Beautitudo.*

Aristotle. *The Eudemian Ethics.*

Aristotle. The *Nicomachean Ethics.*

Csikszentmihaly, M. *Creativity: Flow and the Psychology of Discovery and Invention* (New York: Harper Collins, 1996).

Cutler, Howard and the Dalai Lama. *The Art of Happiness, 10*[th] *Anniversary Edition: A Handbook for Living* (New York: Riverhead Books, 2020).

Excerpt from a speech given by Nelson Mandela at the 90th birthday celebration of Walter Sisulu, Randburg, Johannesburg, South Africa, May 18, 2002.

Frankl, Victor. *Man's Search for Meaning* (Boston: Beacon Press, 2006).

Gallup Poll. 2017.

Gallup Poll. 2018.

Gire, Ken. *Answering the Call: The Doctor Who Made Africa His Life: The Remarkable Story of Albert Schweitzer.* (Nashville: Thomas Nelson, March 18, 2013).

Harvard Business Review. *The Impact of Employee Engagement on Performance.* (Brighton: Harvard Business Publishing, 2013)

History.com Editors. History.com "Buddhism-Definition, Founder and Origins." July 22,2020. https://www.history.com/topics/religion/buddhism.

"Interview with Laurie Santos Today." February 19, 2018.

Lyubomirsky, Sonia. *The How of Happiness: A Scientific Approach to Getting the Life You Want* (New York: Penguin Books, 2007).

Master Class. "How to Shift Your Perspective to Have a Positive Outlook." May 26, 2021. https://www.masterclass.com/articles/how-to-shift-your-perspective-to-have-a-positive-outlook.

Merriman-Webster Dictionary.

McCartney, Sir Paul. "Can't Buy Me Love." 1964.

Michael J. Fox. *Back to the Future* (1, 1985; 2, 1989;3, 1990). United States: Ambelin Entertainment.

Pursuit of Happiness. www.pursuit-of-happiness.org

Saint Rock, Haiti.

Schiraldi, Glenn. *The Resilience Workbook* (Oakland, CA: New Harbinger Publications, 2017).

Seligman, Martin. *Flourish: A Visionary New Understanding of Happiness and Well-Being.* (New York: Free Press, 2011).

Seligman, Martin E.P. *Learned Optimism: How to Change Your Mind and Your Life* (New York: Vintage Books, 2006).

Sossin, W. S. et al. "Neuroscience: A New Pathway to Make Us Smarter and Happier." *Current Biology* 30, no. 18 (2020): R1051-R1054.

Superman. 1, 1978; 2, 1980; 3, 1983; 4, 1987.

Tomasello, Michael et al. "Two Key Steps in the Evolution of Human Cooperation: The Interdependence Hypothesis." *Current Anthropology* 53, no. 6 (November 2012): 673-692.

Travis Roy Foundation. www.travisroyfoundation.org.

Cousins, Norman. *Anatomy of an Illness as Perceived by the Patient* (New York: W.W. Norton & Company, 2005).

Wilson, E. O. *Does Altruism Exist? Culture, Genes and the Welfare of Others* (New Haven: Yale University Press, 2016).

Valliant, G. E. *Aging Well: Surprising Guideposts to a Happier Life from the Landmark Harvard Study of Adult Development* (New York: Little, Brown, 2003).

Santos, Laurie. *PSYC 157: Psychology and the Good Life.* 2018. Coursera.com.

Chapter 13 - PTSD

American Psychiatric Association. *Diagnostic and Statistical Manual of Mental Disorders* (5th edition) (Washington: American Psychiatric Association, 2013): 271-2.

Bienvenu O.J., Gellar J., Althouse B.M., et al., "Post-Traumatic Stress Disorder After Acute Lung Injury: A 2-Year Prospective Longitudinal Study." *Psychological Medicine* 43 (2013): 2657.

Leed, E.J. *No Man's Land: Combat and Identity in World War I* (Cambridge, UK: Cambridge University Press, 1979).

Marshall et al., "Comorbidity, Impairment and Suicidality in Subthreshold PTSD." *American Journal of Psychiatry* 158, no. 9 (September 2001): 1467-73.

Myers, C. S. "A Contribution to the Study of Shell Shock." *The Lancet* 185, no. 4772 (1915): 316-320.

Myers, C.S. "A Contribution to the Study of Shell Shock: Being Account of Certain Cases Treated by Hypnosis." *The Lancet* 1 (1916): 65-69.

Myhren, Hilde, Ekeberg, Oivind, Tøien, Kirsti, Karlsson, Susanne, and Stokland, Karlsson. "Posttraumatic Stress, Anxiety and Depression Symptoms in Patients During the First-Year Post Intensive Care Discharge." *Critical Care* 14, no.1 (2010): R14.

Chapter 14 - Posttraumatic Growth

1993 Nobel Peace Prize, Nelson Mandela.

Resources

1970 Nobel Prize in Literature, Aleksandr Solzhenitsyn.

Arrian. *The Discourses.*

Arrian. *The Enchiridion.*

Brand, Christo and Jone, Barbara. *Doing Life with Mandela: My Prisoner, My Friend.* (Jeppestown, South Africa: Jonathon Ball, 2014).

Clarkson, Kelly. "Stronger (What Doesn't Kill You)." 2012.

Deming, W. Edwards. *Out of Crisis* (Cambridge: MIT Press, October 2018).

Nietzsche, Friedrich. *Twilight of the Idols and the Antichrist: or How to Philosophize with a Hammer* (London: Penguin Classics, 1990).

Hillenbrand, Laura. *Unbroken: A World War II Story of Survival, Resilience and Redemption* (New York: Random House, 2012).

"Letters of Paul to the Romans, 5:3." Bible.

Mandela, Nelson. *Conversations with Myself* (New York: Farrar, Straus and Giroux, 2010).

Mandela, Nelson. *Long Walk to Freedom* (Boston: Little, Brown and Company, 1995).

Mandela, Nelson. *Notes to the Future: Words of Wisdom* (Simon and Schuster, 2012).

Marcus Aurelius. *Meditations.*

Positive Legacy of Trauma." *Journal of Traumatic Stress* 9, no.30 (1996): 455-71.

Seery, Mark D., Holman, E. Alison and Silver, Roxane Cohen. "Whatever Does Not Kill Us: Cumulative Lifetime Adversity, Vulnerability, and Resilience." *Journal Personality and Social Psychology* 20, no.6 (December 2010): 390-394.

Seery, Mark D. "Resilience: A Silver Lining to Experiencing Adverse Life Events." *Journal of Personality and Social Psychology* 99, no. 6 (December 2011): 1025-1041.

Tedeschi, R.G., and Calhoun, L. G. "The Posttraumatic Growth Inventory: Measuring the Positive Legacy of Trauma." *Journal of Traumatic Stress* 9, no. 3 (July 1996): 455-71.

Tedeschi, Richard G. and Moore, Bret A. *The Posttraumatic Growth Workbook* (Oakland: New Harbinger Publications, 2016).

Stockdale, James. *Thoughts of a Philosophical Fighter Pilot.* (Stanford: Hoover Press, 1995).

Solzhenitsyn, Aleksandr. *The Gulag Archipelago: An Experiment in Literary Investigation* (New York: Harper & Row, 1973).

Acknowledgments

How is it possible to adequately acknowledge so many people who saved your life? First and foremost, I will begin with my wife, Colleen. If she had not been awakened during the night by my labored breathing, it is unlikely that I would have been alive in the morning. She got me to South Shore Hospital in time to be placed on life support and made the courageous decision to allow my high-risk transfer during a major blizzard to Brigham and Women's Hospital. This was a pivotal decision that I believe saved my life. She was with me physically and emotionally for the entire illness, which dragged on in stages for over a year. Her devotion to me has gone beyond the bounds of imagination. I owe my life, my recovery, and so much more to Colleen. She is my wife, my best friend, and my soul mate. I will be forever grateful to her.

I want to thank my sons, Michael and Patrick, for dropping everything they had planned in New York City for New Year's Eve 2013 to somehow make the trek through a Raging Nor'easter to be there for me and to support their mother. My brothers James and Paul and my sister Maureen all were amazing in their steadfast and unwavering support of me and in helping to give my wife the breaks she needed to rest and restore herself for the epic battle to save my life then to rebuild it. They were always present, and just hearing their voices helped keep me sane throughout this ordeal. There are no words to express my gratitude. I want to thank my long-deceased father, James Hession, Sr., who gifted me the essential life skills that he had learned to battle through the unimaginable, to steering me to attend Boston College High

School, which was my mother's dream, and then on to Boston College. It was at these schools that I learned so much of what, decades later, helped me process and recover from the trauma that I endured and then to turn that experience into a defining period of my life. I would also like to thank Colleen's parents, Tom and Harriet Hayes (both now deceased), along with her siblings Therese, Peggy, Janet, and Tom, who provided her with unconditional support throughout this ordeal.

I want to thank my close friends Steve and Carol Yamartino, and their children Laura, Caroline, and Stuart. The request that Caroline made as I lay near death for prayers to be said on my behalf at the Grotto to Our Lady of Lourdes on the grounds of Notre Dame, South Bend, Indiana, I truly believe were heard. I want to thank the congregation of Saint Agatha Parish, Milton for their prayers on my behalf. I want to thank our close friends Susan and Everett Hayward for looking after my wife and sons, offering food, a caring ear, and even making travel arrangements for them.

I want to thank Peter Grape, MD and Allen Smith, MD for all the support they gave to me, my wife, and my sons throughout my illness. I also want to thank Richard Whitney, MD, Peter Hoshino, MD, Anthony Marks, MD, Greg Corrodi, MD, Paul Schubert, MD, Seth McClennen, MD, and Susan Feinstein, MD for the support they provided in caring for my patients when I was unable to. I want to thank Denise Reardon, ANP, Hilja Bilodeau, RN, and all of my office nurses and staff for their support and care of my patients and for me. I want to thank Revered Robert Keane, S.J. for helping me find a way to move forward when this seemed impossible.

I want to express my gratitude to the ambulance drivers who got me to South Shore Hospital in time and to the ER staff who stabilized me before being brought to the CCU. I want to thank all the CCU nurses, physicians, and support staff at South Shore Hospital, especially Jon Pehrson, MD, who initiated mechanical life support and Todd Ellerin, MD and Richard Ashburn, MD, who helped walk my wife through the difficult decision to transfer me to BWH. Additionally, I want to thank John Feldman, MD and Robert Driscoll, MD, who cared for me during the myriad setbacks I endured on my long road to recovery. I want to especially thank the brave Boston Med Flight team who transported me to Brigham and Women's Hospital in the face of an impending blizzard.

I am especially grateful to the entire staff of BWH from the ER to the ICU who skillfully brought me back from near death. I want to especially thank the nurses and all those who treated me with not only respect and compassion but as a sentient human being throughout my stay. I would like to thank my physical therapist who never gave up on me, thus helping to make my transfer to Spaulding Hospital possible. I want to thank all of the staff at Spaulding Rehabilitation Hospital, both inpatient and outpatient, who sequentially rebuilt my broken body over many weeks that stretched into months then years. Without their unceasing care, I am not sure that I would have had the favorable outcome that I did.

I want to thank my surgeons at BWH, John Ready, MD, who replaced my hip, Ronald Bleday, MD, and Joel Goldberg, MD, who got me through my abdominal catastrophe. I am forever grateful to them for their skill and compassion.

My long road to recovery would not have been nearly as successful if not for the Sage advice of Janet Lemke, MD to pursue a conservative approach to my back pain and seek dedicated spine physical therapy at Blue Hills Sports and Spine under the direction of Michel Vachon. Without the specialized spine physical therapy that I received it is unlikely that I would be as free from pain as I am and have the mobility that I enjoy.

I owe a special thank you to my editor Tracy Hart for her insight and attention to detail that helped make this book possible.

About the Author

Michael J Hession, MD is a graduate of Boston College High School, Boston College, and Dartmouth Medical School where he was elected to Alpha Omega Alpha. He completed his internal medicine residency at University Hospital (Boston Medical Center) and his cardiovascular fellowship at Brigham and Women's Hospital under Bernard Lown, MD. He is a fellow of the American College of Medicine and the American College of Cardiology. He works as a cardiologist and chief medical officer at Brigham Health Harbor Medical and is an attending physician at South Shore Hospital as well as a consulting physician at Brigham and Women's Hospital in Boston, MA. He has held academic appointments as a clinical instructor in medicine at Harvard Medical School and as an assistant clinical professor of medicine at Tufts Medical School. Eight times he has been included in *Boston Magazine's* Top Doctors annual edition. He lives with his wife of 40 years, Colleen, on Cape Cod, Massachusetts. They enjoy boating on Nantucket Sound, reading, especially history, and traveling—the more exotic, the better.

Dear Readers,

As you turn the final page of *Physician Heal Thyself*, I hope the book has ignited a unique perspective on finding beauty in uncertainty and strength in struggle, inspiring you to embrace every moment with courage and grace.

To continue to draw inspiration from the power of positivity and the art of living fully amidst illness, I invite you to explore my website: www.AcknowledgeAcceptAdapt.com. Here, I offer insights and support to those facing similar issues and to those providing care and companionship to loved ones in their battles.

For daily glimpses into my journey of embracing life to the fullest, follow me on Instagram at @MichaelJHession. Join me in celebrating a life of courage and vitality, navigating through life's toughest challenges with a spirit of hope and adventure.

Warm regards,
Michael J. Hession, MD